MW00633589

GHOSTS & UFOS

Connecting Paranormal Phenomona
through Quantum Physics

adnin lu

Wisdom
Editions

Minneapolis

FIRST EDITION AUGUST 2019
GHOSTS & UFOS: Connecting Paranormal Phenomena through
Quantum Physics.

Copyright © 2019 by Adrian Lee. All rights reserved.

No part of this book may be used or reproduced in any manner
whatsoever without written permission except in the case of brief
quotations used in critical articles and reviews. Wisdom Editions is an
imprint of Calumet Editions, LLC. For information, write to Calumet
Editions, 8422 Rosewood Drive, Chanhassen, MN 55317

Printed in the United States of America.
10 9 8 7 6 5 4 3 2 1

ISBN: 978-1-950743-12-4

Cover design: Adrian Lee
Interior design: Gary Lindberg

Back cover photographs in descending order:

Scratched by an unseen hand in Jackson, Minnesota.
An orb in the boiler room of Morton School, Renville County, Minnesota.
Stefan Michalak recovering in hospital from radiation burns after his UFO encounter.

If you want to prove extraordinary things like ghosts and UFOs, you have to use extraordinary thinking.

Contents

Also by Adrian Lee

How to be a Christian Psychic: What the Bible Says about Mediums, Healers and Paranormal Investigators

Mysterious Midwest: Unwrapping Urban Legends and Ghostly Tales from the Dead

Mysterious Minnesota: Digging Up the Ghostly Past at Thirteen Haunted Sites

GHOSTS & UFOS

Connecting Paranormal Phenomona through Quantum Physics

ADRIAN LEE

Wisdom
Editions

Minneapolis, Minnesota

Foreword

Adrian has blasted this whole thing wide open!

My fascination with ufology started as a child—inspired by an infectiously enthusiastic high school teacher with a passion for UFOs. Many years later a chance meeting with the same teacher rekindled my need to find answers to the mysteries of the universe. I immersed myself in the subject and soon became a field investigator for the Mutual UFO Network MUFON—I eventually became the State Director for MUFON of Minnesota.

In my experience, MUFON has traditionally focused on the narrow study of UFOs. Meeting topics are normally limited to the nuts and bolts study of unidentified vehicles. Bigfoot, crop circles, animal mutilations, and alien abductions were once taboo and never uttered in the same sentence as the term UFO. Talk of UFOs being inter-dimensional, ultra-dimensional, or extra-dimensional, would be frowned upon. So to even suggest that ghosts and UFOs could be interlinked would be heresy!

I then invited ghost hunter Adrian Lee to attend a MUFON meeting to give a presentation on UFOs in Renaissance Art. As founder of The International Paranormal Society, he brought a wealth of knowledge gained from a lifetime of investigating haunted locations. He invited me to accompany his team, and I was thoroughly impressed. The paranormal investigators used the same equipment, objective eye and forensic techniques in scrutinizing the evidence as the ufologist. The team then invited me to join full time, and I have now seen as fact the phenomena of ghosts and UFOs—and both are real!

The question should no longer be, *do you believe in ghosts and UFOs?* But, rather, how good is the evidence that ghosts and UFOs exist. I have seen Adrian Lee's theories and ideas evolve and develop with every UFO encounter and ghostly contact. Not only does Adrian Lee present the strongest evidence that both exist, but he uniquely presents how they exist.

Lorna J. Hunter
Former Minnesota State Director for MUFON

Preface

I am the founder of The International Paranormal Society and a member of the Luton Paranormal Society in England. I have investigated ghosts and paranormal activity all over the world. I first became interested in the paranormal after experiencing several events in my childhood home. The idea progressively evolved that I could interface with the dead for historical purposes.

I first came to Minnesota early in 2008 to work on several paranormal video productions and spent two years working in Minneapolis as the national and international news correspondent for a live paranormal talk radio show on 100.3 KTLK. I currently host the only weekly paranormal news quiz show, *More Questions than Answers*, every Friday on the Dark Matter Digital Radio Network.

Clairvoyance informs my paranormal investigations. I often see in my third eye detailed pictures presented by the deceased. This allows me to have very precise communication with the spirits. I also have the skills of remote viewing and clairsentience. As a boy my psychic sensitivities were dormant; it was only through my work with other "sensitives" and through being exposed to various kinds of paranormal contact—coupled with my own personal psychic development—that I developed to where I can now utilize those skills freely. Like any other ability, my clairvoyance continues to evolve and becomes stronger through the implementation of a design for life, critical introspection, and practice.

I have written the following books: *Mysterious Minnesota, Digging up the Ghostly Past at Thirteen Haunted Sites*; *How to be a Christian Psychic: What the Bible says about Mediums, Healers and Paranormal Investigators*; and *Mysterious Midwest, Unwrapping Urban Legends and Ghostly Tales from the Dead*. I currently lecture on all aspects of the paranormal, including ghosts, UFOs, psychic development and angels.

My qualifications are in art history and the study of history methodologies. As an art historian, with a specialist background in the early Renaissance period, I sometimes found UFOs depicted in European paintings from the fourteenth to sixteenth centuries. I tried to understand why these images were depicted, taking into consideration the political and contractual issues surrounding the painting of Biblical scenes on church walls. The church clearly saw benefit in recognizing these UFOs in the costly frescos. Clearly, the local peasantry was observing these vehicles from the fields in which they worked. The painters, depicting these objects as divine and sent by God, undoubtedly sought to remove questioning of the church, suppressing what the church simply couldn't answer.

Former MUFON State Director Lorna Hunter asked me to present a talk on UFOs in Renaissance Art to MUFON members at its annual symposium in Minneapolis. She also invited me onto a question and answer forum with several top ufologists. I was embarrassed that the audience wanted to hear more about ghosts than UFOs. As I fielded questions, with UFO experts interjecting their opinions, I realized that the two fields of investigation were overlapping; I could apply my theories on ghostly phenomena to the canon of ufology. Thus began the project you now see before you. It was a long and sometimes overwhelming journey. The research, history, facts, psychology, philosophy and contemporary scientific theory stretched me like no other book had. But to paraphrase Theodore Roosevelt (1858–1919), *nothing in the world is worth having or worth doing unless it means effort, pain, and difficulty…*

Introduction

My first paranormal investigation started in a haunted community hall in Bedfordshire, England. I cautiously explored the building with a historian's mindset; I was not willing to believe ghostly activity had occurred unless I could prove it. Now, over two decades later, I can claim that ghosts exist—I have seen them, spoken to them, interviewed them, embraced them, recorded them, photographed them, flirted with them, laughed with them, and written about them. Some have even attacked me! I work with them every day in some capacity, and they provide messages and valuable information. I have written two critically acclaimed history books on Minnesota and the Midwest with lost historical information ghosts have provided.

I also believe in UFOs and alien life on other planets in our universe. I have observed incredible and multiple UFO sightings. I have captured them on video, photographed them, interviewed people who have seen them and witnessed the trace evidence they leave behind.

I started to establish my ideas for this book over eight years ago. It was a project that continued in the background as I completed other books for which I conducted numerous paranormal investigations and gained deep knowledge about some of the most haunted buildings in the world. During these eight years, I also had the opportunity to witness several prominent and historically important UFO sightings. This primary evidence would prove a key to my theories.

If you search through the recorded archives of the US government, you will find many documented accounts throughout the latter half of the twentieth century proclaiming that UFOs exist. As President Harry S. Truman declared on April 4, 1950, at a press conference:

> I can assure you that, given they exist, these flying saucers are made by no power on this Earth.

At the end of 2017, the US Government Defense Department acknowledged the existence of its long-secret UFO investigation program that was started in 2007 with a twenty-two-million-dollar budget. Due to increasing financial restraints, the project closed, and the admission of its existence proclaimed some astonishing statements. Luis Elizondo, the former head of the Pentagon program to understand the mysteries of UFOs, presided over the Advanced Aviation Threat Identification Program. Elizondo stated that UFOs visiting Earth had been "Proved beyond reasonable doubt" and "unidentified flying objects of advanced capabilities had been seen 'lots' over the years." He continued, "I think it's pretty clear this is not us, and it's not anyone else, so one has to ask the question where they're from."

The program investigated issues that sounded like ideas from a science fiction movie. They included wormholes and warp drives, as well as interviewing pilots and military personnel who had reported experiences with UFOs. Elizondo said that many of the Navy pilots described aircraft moving and acting in a way that seemed to be beyond human beings' current capabilities. He said, "We had never seen anything like it."

These uniquely overt statements provide two astonishing facts: that many high-ranking people in the federal government believe aliens have visited Planet Earth and that military pilots have recorded videos of UFOs with capabilities that seem to outstrip all known human aircraft, such as changing direction and accelerating in ways no fighter jet or helicopter could ever accomplish.

The Pentagon openly acknowledged the fate of the program in response to a Reuters query, but the Pentagon was less clear about whether the UFO program continues to hover somewhere in the vast universe of the US defense establishment. According to its backers, the program remains in existence and officials continue to investigate UFO episodes brought to their attention by service members.

Days after this revelation, *The New York Times* published a story that revealed the US Government's stockpile of alloys and other materials believed to be associated with UFOs. The Defense Department, in a building complex in Las Vegas, has a cache of materials described as being *from out of this world*. Times reporter Ralph Blumenthal stated, "They have, as we reported in the paper, some material from these objects that is being studied so that scientists can find what accounts for their amazing properties, this technology of these objects, whatever they are." When asked what the materials were, Blumenthal responded, "They don't know. They're studying it, but it's some kind of compound that they don't recognize."

At the end of February 2018, the British press revealed that the Pentagon held files that showed secret agents were researching the threats posed by UFOs. The papers written between 2007 and 2012 reported, "Metals unknown to science had been recovered, tested, and placed into a private facility." Ufologists have long believed metals existed from alien crash sites, such as the infamous Roswell incident of 1947.

The British Department of Defense spent some of its sixteen-million-pound UFO budget to contract Bigelow Aerospace in Las Vegas. Files found under Robert Bigelow's direction in the company's headquarters showed buildings *modified* to allow the storage of the materials. James Oberg, a former NASA employee said:

> The money went out of the Department of Defense
> to Robert Bigelow, and he contracted the work out
> to some UFO groups to look for UFOs and who

spent a lot of money retrofitting his buildings to store this material.

Nick Pope, a former investigator of UFOs for the British Ministry of Defense, also believes UFO groups that investigate alien activities took parts and kept a database of sightings. He added:

> We don't know how these alloys and other materials were obtained. We're told they relate to UFOs, and if they come from some sort of military encounter, this is potentially very significant. However, we also know that Bigelow Aerospace acquired all sorts of UFO-related materials from civilian UFO research groups.

Revelations such as these placed this book into a sharper focus. With an increase in the public's thirst for knowledge, and with more government information revealed on a weekly basis, my publisher suggested I bring this project to the fore. After eight years of attending and giving MUFON lectures, talking and sharing ideas with prominent ufologists, experiencing my own UFO encounters and sightings, sitting in haunted buildings for endless hours, avidly reading and searching through data, books, reports and audio recordings, I now believe ghosts and UFOs are linked together in some incredible ways and that two of the greatest mysteries in the canon of human existence could be placed together in one book. All I had to do was write it! To quote the great Rod Serling—screenwriter, playwright, and presenter of *The Twilight Zone*—"Coming up with ideas is the easiest thing on earth. Putting them down is the hardest."

Skeptics may disagree with the ideas and concepts I'm about to present; history will be my judge. That is why I back up my ideas with primary and secondary evidence and resource material, scientific fact and sound theories worthy of consideration. Remember, if you want to prove extraordinary things like ghosts and UFOs, you need to do some extraordinary thinking.

In this book I will highlight how UFOs and ghosts have interacted with mankind for millennia in various ways and how we have documented and responded to those interactions through pictorial evidence, the written word, and popular culture. I will deal with commonalities—including behavior, actions, modes of transport and movement, and use of energy—as well as the paranormal abilities they exhibit. I will also discuss theories on how and why these phenomena exist based on personal experiences and through extensive research within the field of the paranormal, psychology, philosophy, and contemporary quantum theory.

The Need for Progressive Thinking

Ghost rocket sightings in Sweden during peacetime soon followed the Foo Fighter UFO encounters during the last years of the Second World War. These phenomena prompted a burgeoning interest in ufology at the end of the 1940s as a specific area of study for the government, and by default the military. Governments around the world worried that other nations had developed greater weapons technology than their own. The Soviet Union came under great scrutiny as a source of the ghost rocket sightings.

A secret dossier revealed in the summer of 2018 showed that British spies spent fifty years trying to catch a UFO in order to use its alien technology to build superweapons. Declassified files have shown that the British government was concerned about the Soviet Union and China impounding UFOs and harvesting their secrets to develop super-fast warplanes.

A one-thousand-page report called UAPs (Unidentified Aerial Phenomena) in the UK Air Defense Region, has been recently declassified. The document reveals how the RAF expressed a great interest in finding a UFO to help them come up with an innovative way of beating enemies during the Cold War. An RAF air chief was *particularly interested in any novel technologies which might be useful to their programs.* Another air force commander feared the enemy may have already seized a UFO, writing: "Monitor all reports in case in the future the hitherto unknown/not understood underlying phenomena is being exploited by another nation. An actual - or potential enemy - could develop a flying device with the characteristics that these phenomena seem to have."

Spies also received tips on what to look for when identifying foreign objects. An unnamed commander wrote: "Particular attention should be paid to any aircraft behaving 'like a UFO.' Look out for high velocities, sharp maneuvers, stationary "flight," and few radar returns."

Further acknowledgment of UFOs during the Second World War came when newly released files accused Sir Winston Churchill of covering up a close encounter between an RAF aircraft and a UFO. The former prime minister allegedly ordered the unexplained incident over the east coast of England to remain secret for at least fifty years, as he believed it would cause mass panic.

The National Archives made the declassified Ministry of Defense UFO files available online, and allegations of the cover-up then emerged. A scientist from Leicester wrote to the government in 1999 looking for more information about the incident. He described how his grandfather, who served with the RAF during the war, was present when Churchill and General Dwight Eisenhower discussed how to deal with the UFO encounter.

The man, unnamed in the files, said Churchill reportedly exclaimed, "This event should be immediately classified, since it would create mass panic amongst the general population and destroy one's belief in the church." The incident allegedly involved an RAF reconnaissance plane returning from a mission in France toward the end of the war. The plane was over the English coastline when a strange metallic object matched the aircraft's course and speed before accelerating away and disappearing.

Neither side was able to match a plausible explanation to these observations—this caused a high degree of concern. During the discussion with Churchill, a consultant working in Cumbria dismissed the possibility of the object being a missile since missiles could not suddenly match the aircraft's speed and then accelerate.

Another person at the meeting raised the possibility of an unidentified flying object, at which point Churchill declared the incident classified for fifty years for review by future prime ministers. In 1947 the British intelligence services decided to begin operating two UFO desks. Whitehall eventually closed these projects in 1997, stating that the investigation of aliens, sightings, and abductions diverted from its main duties.

Dr. David Clarke, author of *The UFO Files* and senior lecturer in journalism from Sheffield Hallam University, reviewed the declassified files from 1947 to 1997 and commented on a change in attitude. "These papers demonstrate how far official policy towards UFOs changed after the Cold War," he wrote. "In 1997 the Ministry of Defense was no longer interested in UFOs as a defense problem, but as a purely public relations issue. This inevitably led to the closure of the public UFO hotline at the end of 2009."

The Birth of Ufology

With reports of UFOs both during and after the Second World War, and with a myriad of motives, this new area of study was underway with the unrealistic expectation there would soon be an explanation for UFO sightings. Yet, as we find ourselves firmly planted in the twenty-first century, assiduity has waned. The answers were not forthcoming, and the dreams of ufologists to study alien vehicle nuts and bolts have all but disappeared.

Top ufologist and author Kevin Randle reinforces this idea in a 2011 interview in the *Skeptical Inquirer* publication:

> We said this field has not progressed in over twenty years. It's now been another ten or twelve years, and it still has not progressed. I set a very high bar for the level of evidence required. There are very few authentic UFO cases. However, some skeptical explanations don't fit the facts. Still, I'm getting more skeptical in my old age.

One theory of why these kinds of sightings have disappeared is that the clichéd stereotypical saucer shapes prevalent in the public consciousness of the 1950s are no longer in contemporary thinking. Even the documenting of alien's wearing their own climate-controlled spacesuits have disappeared from reports. The saturation of over seventy years of television and film depictions of the classically styled UFO have familiarized us with a visual UFO language. Their form has become a cliché, and so we no longer experience the same shock or fear when seeing one. The result is apathy in reporting cases.

MUFON data now traditionally presents the majority of recorded sightings as various forms of balls and strange lights:

Shape of Object	No. of Reports
Sphere	195
Circle	127
Star-like	125
Other	90
Oval	72
Triangle	72
Disc	72
Unknown	67
Fireball	59
Cylinder	50
Flash	30
Boomerang	30
Cigar	23
Diamond	16
Egg	15
Bullet/Missile	14
Blimp	12
Saturn-like	10
Teardrop	10
Chevron	9
Cone	6
Cross	5

(Data from the month of October 2013:)

With more people looking to the skies, and with more ways to film and record sightings, aliens may have responded by changing, masking, or cloaking their appearance to remain undetected. Another theory suggests that sightings from the late 1940s to the 1960s were our own vehicles. When the earth-based projects and development stopped, so did the sightings. Whatever the reason, contact cases involving physical vehicles are less frequent than in the 1950s and 1960s.

The Psychology of Perception

In the 1940s and 1950s we knew of the aluminum sheet metal construction of aircraft, like the B-17 Flying Fortress bomber. It is possible, then, that we psychologically made a connection in our minds to how we believed UFOs must have been constructed. In modern society we have a better knowledge and understanding of energy and light, so we are able to process a sighting more easily. We only understand what we see at any given time in history through the lens of previous knowledge, which gives us context to draw upon. This explains why balls of energy were often mistaken for angels during the fifteenth century.

Joseph Banks was a botanist on Captain James Cook's 1770 voyage to Australia. Banks documented that natives paid virtually no attention to the 106-foot-long *Endeavour* when traveling close to the coastline. On April 28, while sailing north along the east coast of Australia, he recorded in his diary the lack of reaction by local fishermen:

> Seemd to be totaly engag'd in what they were about: the ship passd within a quarter of a mile of them and yet they scarce lifted their eyes from their employment.

Banks seemed confused at their lack of acknowledgement:

> Not one was once observd to stop and look toward the ship; they pursued their way in all appearance intirely unmovd by the neighbourhood of so

remarkable an object as a ship must necessarily be
to people who have never seen one.

When the explorers attempted to land in their longboats,
however, the natives resisted:

> ... As soon as we aproachd the rocks two of the men
> came down upon them, each armd with a lance.

When presented with a new experience it is difficult to
comprehend visual information when we have no frame of reference
based on previous exposure. The early Renaissance artist Masaccio
painted a fresco of the Holy Trinity in 1425 on the wall of the
Dominican church of Santa Maria Novella in Florence. It is unique
in depicting the crucifixion of Christ in one of the first examples
of linear perspective—the illusion of showing a three-dimensional
architectural scene on a flat two-dimensional surface with the use of
vanishing points and a horizon.

Masaccio, *Holy Trinity*, c. 1427, Fresco,
667 x 317 cm, Santa Maria Novella, Florence.

The congregation was shocked to witness the illusion of depth depicted on the wall. Their perception of depth was not as developed as ours. We now grow up in a modern visual environment with toys and electronic stimuli that allow us to understand a three-dimensional world. The congregation allegedly walked around to the outside of the church looking to find the added extension, such was the illusion of depth. Within our own era you may have experienced this phenomenon with the introduction of holograms in the 1970s and 1980s. You may recall touching the two-dimensional surface to convince your brain the image was actually flat.

If we do not introduce new ideas and concepts into the canon of ufology, stagnation will prevail. Any ufologist that wishes to stick to the nuts and bolts study of UFOs will be reduced to the retrospective researching of old cases from the 1950s and 1960s because the study of ufology does not exist in the same way as it once did.

Some members of the ufology community would balk at the prospect of embracing ideas brought from other paranormal perspectives, as this would take the study of UFOs away from the narrow pedagogical path they wish to see, perhaps believing it to be an unnecessary distraction. I believe it would be an opportunity missed if the ufologist did not consider other forms of paranormal thinking. Remember, a ball of energy in the sky is a UFO, but a ball of energy in the basement is an orb!

Facts We Can Rely On

The phenomena of ghosts and UFOs are interlinked together and with humanity. The following are facts that can be relied upon.

When I first started to formulate my ideas in connecting ghosts with UFOs, I saw the same forensic techniques and data retrieval structures utilized by both the paranormal investigator and the ufologist. I found the data collection sheets to be almost identical in recording the time of day, the temperature, and other weather-related data. Also documented by both were the competencies of the eyewitnesses, from their perceived mental states to whether alcohol or drugs may have played a part. Both disciplines share the same objective eye when scrutinizing the evidence. Equipment cases also bulge with similar tools and devices, from the humble flashlight to the electromagnetic field (EMF) meters, laser pens, thermometers, cameras, thermal imaging devices, infrared technology, audio recording equipment, and the obligatory notepad and pen.

UFOs Have Tracked Mankind for Millennia

The historical development and recording of both ghosts and UFOs have followed similar paths. Both phenomena have been with us and part of human culture from the moment we gained language and a sentient awareness of ourselves. Barbara Lamb, MS, MFT, CHT, documented in a 2007 article, *The Big Picture of Extraterrestrial Contact Experiences & How Regression Therapy Can Help,* how the interaction between aliens and humans has taken place over thousands of years and how contact is more prolific than we imagined:

> Many ancient sources indicate interaction between extraterrestrial beings (who seem to come from the heavens or space) and humans for thousands of years. In recent times, contacts and abductions have been reported since the early 1960s. According to polls taken during the 1980s and 1990s an estimated five to eight million Americans have had these experiences, and it is a world-wide phenomenon as well. Since 1991, when I first worked with a traumatized extraterrestrial experiencer client, I have regressed more than 500 people to various experiences of extraterrestrial contact—perhaps 1500 regressions. I am currently working with 15 abductees, and I lead a monthly support group for experiencers as well.

Elaine Douglass, MS, was an experienced UFO researcher and author. During her career she became the MUFON state director for both Utah and Washington DC. During the 1990s she was an organizer for Operation Right to Know (ORTK), an organization that sponsored public protests against UFO secrecy. In her essay *The breaking of Jim Sparks, or why the aliens don't land on the White House lawn*, Douglass transcribes the experiences of an abductee called Jim Sparks who is informed by aliens that his family has been tracked for millennia:

> Now Jim is given the "answer" to his question, Why me? Jim is told the aliens have been keeping track of his family line for 2 million years, and Jim believes it. The story is conveyed in a holographic slide show. Scene one depicts WWII and one of the characters "looks just like me!" Jim writes

excitedly. "That chin, that nose, those dark eyes and brows, they were just like mine! The hair was even curly…"

Next is a Victorian-era scene with another character who looks just like Jim! Now a scene from the fifteenth century and another guy who "looked just like me…"

John Carpenter, MSW, LCSW, obtained a Bachelor of Arts degree in Psychology from DePauw University, Indiana, and has a Master's degree in Social Work from Washington University, St. Louis. He practices as a psychiatric therapist and hypnotherapist in Branson, Missouri. Carpenter has volunteered his services to investigating many hundreds of possible UFO abductions. He states in his essay *Which alien agenda is it?* that aliens have been making contact with mankind for thousands of years with the effect of stimulating human evolution through education and spiritual growth.

This may have been a factor in the past as a review of ancient civilizations indicates that our ancestors often knew more than they should have or could have been capable of knowing. For example, how could ancient civilizations have known about planets and star systems that could not yet be observed with the naked eye or with any known telescopic devices? The Sumerians were amazingly advanced in many fields of knowledge, but also talked of beings coming from the sky to share this information with them. Many cultures tell of people coming from the sky and educating them.

The Documentation of Early Contact

Passed down through generations by oral tradition are the stories of strange encounters with lights or unknown objects in the sky, often believed to be the work of the gods. Marked by percussive blows, blood or charcoal, cave walls displayed pictorial documentation showing many mythical and mystical beings that appeared to descend from the heavens.

These earliest images have led many scholars, like Erich von Däniken, to believe the ancients documented their encounters with UFOs and aliens in a formalistic way. The paintings found in the ancient caves of Peche Merle, France, the petroglyphs located in Val Camonica, Italy, and the images of aliens believed to be Wondjina gods depicted by the Australian Aborigines in 6000 BC are all good examples. They were created in cultural isolation of one another at different times in history.

The Greek historian Diodorus Siculus, who told the story of General Timoleon witnessing a "torch in the sky" as he sailed his fleet from Greece to Sicily in 343 BC, recorded one of the earliest written descriptions of a UFO. The Roman historian Titus Livius (Livy) also reported seeing "ships" that shone in the sky over Rome in 214 BC. From the Medieval era through to the Baroque period we continue to see the pictorial documentation of strange aerial craft. The *Madonna and Child with the Infant St. John* attributed to Sebatiano Mainardi in the late fifteenth century and the *Glorification of the Eucharist* by Bonaventura Salimbeni in 1600 are two good examples.

The first use of the word "Starship" came in the 1882 book *Oahspe: A New Bible* by John Ballou Newbrough. Martians fired capsules towards Earth in the 1898 novel *The War of the Worlds* by H.G. Wells. Early films of the twentieth century presented alien life and ufology with *Flash Gordon* in 1936 and *Buck Rogers* in 1939. The tradition continued with *E.T. the Extra-Terrestrial* in 1982 and on to the medium of television with aliens depicted in shows like *The Jetsons* in 1962 and the sitcom *ALF* in 1986.

Ghosts and Spirits with Us from the Beginning

The concepts of ghosts and spirits have arguably been part of the human psyche from the moment we climbed out of the trees and gained an awareness of ourselves and our place in the world. You could not recognize the ghost of your mother for what it is if you have no awareness of what a mother is and who we are in relation to her.

Our earliest ancestors embraced the idea that we come back in spirit after death to interact with the living. According to the ancient Indonesian Torajan belief system, spirits walk the earth which provides the foundation for a common ritual called *Ma'nene,* or the *ceremony of cleaning corpses.* If a person died on a journey, the family would go to the place of death and then accompany the deceased home by walking the corpse back to the village. Tribal members were afraid to journey far from home in case they died and were unable to return.

Some of the earliest recorded ghostly encounters in Western European society were documented by the Roman historian Tacitus and the Roman letter writer Pliny the Younger. Another early source documenting the concept of ghosts and spirits is the Bible. King Saul raised the ghost of Samuel in 1 Samuel, and in Luke 24:39 Jesus tells his disciples *he is not a ghost.* Jesus also takes three of his disciples to the mountains and allows them to witness His interaction with the ghosts of Moses and Elijah in Matthew 17.

One of the earliest examples of poltergeist activity comes from a story called the *Drummer of Tedworth,* a tale about a home plagued by ghostly nocturnal drumming noises caused by a mischievous spirit. Joseph Glanvill documented this in his book *Saducismus Triumphatus* in 1668. Glanvill told of a local landowner called John Mompesson who owned a house in Tedworth, now Tidworth in Wiltshire, England. He brought a lawsuit against a local drummer accused of extorting money from him. After the legal ruling went against the drummer, his drum was confiscated. Mompesson then found his home plagued by drumming noises. The assumption was the drummer had brought about this macabre action by way of witchcraft.

In more modern times a set of conventions dictated what a ghost should look like and how it should behave. This falsely learned knowledge derived from a wide range of fictional media including the books and plays of William Shakespeare, Oscar Wilde and Charles Dickens, who provided us with the white, chain-rattling, groaning ghost in the novel *A Christmas Carol* in 1843. Dickens described the apparition:

> Marley's face... had a dismal light about it, like a bad lobster in a dark cellar. Marley also has a bandage under his chin, tied at the top of his head, ... how much greater was his horror, when the phantom taking off the bandage round its head, as if it were too warm to wear indoors, its lower jaw dropped down upon its breast!

With the advent of the motion picture, followed closely by the medium of television, the screen depictions of ghosts became common and spanned a variety of genres, the first being *Scrooge* or *Marley's Ghost*, a short British film from 1901 that adapted the tale of a *Christmas Carol*. Another early cinematic depiction of a ghost came from 1915 in the American silent film *Ghost*. Many ghost-themed films then hit the silver screen throughout the 1930s and '40s. There was the ghost and castle relocation from Scotland to Florida in the British comedy *The Ghost Goes West*, which was voted the best British film of 1935. The trend continued with *A Matter of Life and Death* in 1946 and *The Ghost and Mrs. Muir* in 1947, continuing to the 1980s *Ghostbusters* film franchise and the celebrated 1990 film *Ghost*. Children's benevolent ghost stories also became popular, such as *Casper the Friendly Ghost* created in the 1930s. Casper appeared in comics, animated cartoons and eventually the 1995 feature film *Casper*. Television also introduced *Randall and Hopkirk (deceased)*, a 1969 British series depicting a private detective helped by the ghost of his partner.

Do We Know Any More about Them?

Despite thousands of documented years of interactions and experiences with both UFOs and ghosts, we still know hardly anything about either. In London, a collective of scholars and scientists for the exploration and study of paranormal activity founded *The Society for Psychical Research* in 1882. This society represented one of the first attempts at correlating and evaluating information collected on paranormal phenomena. This enthusiasm for finding answers about the afterlife continued into the twentieth century with British psychic researcher Henry Price. Price created great interest in his well-publicized investigations, including his work at the infamously haunted Borley Rectory in Essex, England, from 1937 to 1938. The techniques and methodologies he employed have not changed greatly since his time.

The east face of Borley Rectory in 1892.

Paranormal investigating has only moved forward in the last one hundred and thirty years through the introduction of new technology. Recording on magnetic tape has been replaced with digital voice recorders. Military technological advancements have drip-fed affordable and accessible thermal imaging cameras and infrared technology into the marketplace. Digital photography, audio technology, video and thermal imaging recorders, apps and tools aid in the process of documenting and connecting us with extraterrestrial activity and the spirit world. Yet we are no further to knowing what UFOs and ghosts are.

Our quest to prove these phenomena are real, through the use of technology, stems from the belief that if science cannot provide proof, then it must not exist. But science always struggles to keep up with man's wisdom, and scientific technology is not yet available to prove beyond a doubt that ghosts or UFOs exist. Before 1992 we believed only nine planets existed—those found within our solar system. We have now documented over a thousand planets in the universe, and the number increases weekly. Predictions now suggest that four-hundred billion planets are in the Milky Way. That does not mean those planets did not exist before 1992, just that earlier science could not prove they existed.

Science Can Be Wrong

Scientists once labelled certain phenomena impossible which later turned out to be true. They disbelieved, for example, what the theory of relativity now confirms. And who would have thought that randomness would play any role in fundamental physical laws? Given its evolving nature, scientists are sometimes wrong about the implications and limitations of their discoveries. What I wish to highlight are ways contemporary science is starting to challenge old theories to provide ideas that could account for the way ghosts and UFOs behave.

Current Science Will Not Solve These Problems

Observations over the last one hundred years show that subatomic entities, like electrons and photons, behave in pellet-like particles or waves. But when we attempt to observe their behavior using measuring instruments, they appear as particles. When the instrumentation is removed they once again appear as waves, meaning they don't seem to be located in any specific point in space at any given moment. They are literally dependent on the presence of the mind to attain a position in three-dimensional reality. So if ghosts are made of electrons and photons, *it would require a mind to make them exist,* and they would exist in every part of the universe at any given time. This would also be a useful mechanism to harness by extraterrestrials when trying to traverse the universe.

From this quantum perspective, the human mind and consciousness creates and sustains what seems like a universe independent of and much vaster and older than ourselves. Mainstream scientists are profoundly uncomfortable with such mystical viewpoints. They dismiss and deride the idea of spirits, ghosts, psychic powers, reincarnation, heaven, hell, angels, demons, and other invisible immaterial entities. This is partly because they are associated with the medieval European past when the suppression of reason led to atrocities like witch hunts, the Spanish Inquisition, and the demonization of mental illness.

Science, by its own definition, is the investigation of one domain—the observable material world. A scientist who only investigates one domain of phenomena by default should not claim other domains do not exist. It's one thing to say, "I'm only going to explore the Atlantic Ocean." But you cannot then claim no other oceans exist, and you are crazy if you think they do. It is bad science to say, "No observations, except the kinds that I make, are possible." In the same way, of course, ufologists may choose to ignore and resist paranormal explanations for UFOs.

By definition, science has limited itself to one realm of exploration. This means there is no logical or scientific basis for it to make comments about other possible realms. New possibilities are always hard to believe until we invent or discover them. Many things we now take for granted were impossible to believe in our grandparents' era. Everything we take for granted as an absolute and incontrovertible fact is subject to being overturned in the future.

Traveling Through Walls

Science dictates that mass cannot travel through walls. By default, then, ghosts cannot be a mass or exhibit weight. If ghosts can walk through walls, they are not comprised of particles at that moment. Even light in the form of an orb would not be able to pass through solid matter because light is composed of particles called photons.

Some waves can pass through matter, though. Gamma rays travel through solid objects and so do radio waves, energy at either end of the electromagnetic spectrum. These waves are examples of electromagnetic (EM) radiation. Three things happen to EM radiation when it encounters a barrier: it can bounce—called reflectance or scattering; it can pass through—called transmittance; or it just plain stops—called absorbance. Gamma rays can pass through solid matter as the rays are too small and fast to interact with the matter. Radio waves are too large and slow to interact with solid matter so can also pass through.

Several break-through discoveries in the field of quantum physics in the last twelve months have challenged the conventional thinking we have discussed, and scientists have been proven wrong in the areas of light becoming mass, massless particles, and the ability of matter to travel through mass.

Particles Passing Through a Mass

Contemporary science now says particles can actually pass through solid matter under the right circumstances. This process is quantum tunneling and occurs when a particle passes through a barrier. Scientists have measured electrons escaping from atoms without having the energy to do so. This is comparable to jumping through a wall.

Quantum tunneling is possible because of the wave nature of matter. In the quantum world, particles often act likes waves of water rather than billiard balls. This means an electron doesn't exist in a single place at a single time with a single energy, but rather as a wave of probabilities. Scientists forced an electron to tunnel out of an atom and measured the moment to within two hundred attoseconds. These findings could help scientists understand other super-fast processes that rely on quantum tunneling.

Massless Particles

Researchers only recently confirmed the existence of a massless particle called the Weyl fermion, which has the unique ability to behave as both matter and antimatter inside a crystal. This strange particle can create electrons that have no mass. The existence of this particle is huge because it paves the way for much more efficient electronics and new types of quantum computing. Weyl fermions could solve the electron traffic jams that occur in today's electronics because they move in a more efficient, ordered way than electrons.

The universe is made of fermions and bosons. Fermions are the building blocks that make up all matter, such as electrons. Bosons are the particles that carry force, such as photons. Fermions are more efficient than electrons because the particle's spin is simultaneously in the same direction as its motion. This means all fermions move in exactly the same way and can traverse through and around obstacles that scatter normal electrons.

It is believed that fermions have their own GPS, helping them to steer themselves without scattering. They move in one direction and never come to a stop because they just keep tunneling through. Weyl fermions are quasiparticles, which means they can only exist in a solid such as a crystal; they cannot exist as stand-alone particles. Further research will help scientists work out just how useful they could be. The physics of the Weyl fermion is so strange that many possibilities that we are incapable of imagining right now could arise from these particles.

Creating Matter from Light

The example above proves that particles can pass through solid matter. I now want to show that light can have physical qualities.

Physicists at Imperial College in London have recently discovered how to create matter from light, a feat thought impossible eighty years ago. New research published in *Nature Photonics* shows this theory is provable. A photon-photon collider imagined by the physicists would convert light directly into matter using technology that is already available, presenting a new type of high-energy physics experiment.

The collider experiment proposed by the scientists involves two key steps. First, the scientists would use a high-intensity laser to accelerate electrons to nearly the speed of light. They would then fire these electrons into a slab of gold to create a beam of photons a billion times more energetic than visible light. The second stage of the experiment involves a tiny gold can called a hohlraum. Scientists would fire a high-energy laser at the inner surface of this gold can to create a thermal radiation field generating light similar to the light emitted by stars. They would then direct the photon beam from the first stage of the experiment through the center of the can, causing the photons from the two sources to collide and form electrons and positrons. Physicists believe it would then be possible to detect the formation of the electrons and positrons when they exited the can.

Light Can Be Solid

A recent breakthrough discovery from researchers at the Harvard-MIT Center for Ultracold Atoms, have discovered how to make individual photons interact and bind together into molecular structures creating a completely new state of matter. This could potentially allow light molecules to form solid structures. This is good news for all *Star Wars* fans that want real lightsabers!

While this discovery blows the roof off the traditional understanding of light, it didn't come out of nowhere. Theories about the possibility for these strange types of bound photonic states have existed for some time but have been impossible to test. A 1905 paper by Albert Einstein put forward the idea that light consists of localized packets of energy (quanta), giving it a particle-like property.

To get the photons to interact, researchers took atoms of rubidium and put them into a specialized vacuum chamber capable of cooling the atoms to an ultra-cold temperature. They then used a laser to fire individual photons into the frozen cloud of atoms. As the photons passed through the medium they slowed down. By the time they exited the medium they had bound together.

The reason the photons bind together is due to something called a Rydberg blockade. Basically, as the photons pass through the cold medium, they trade off exiting nearby atoms, effectively acting in tandem to clear a path for one another. It's a photonic interaction mediated by the atomic interaction that makes these two photons behave like a molecule. When they exit the medium, they're much more likely to bind together than emerge as single photons. A potential application for this phenomenon is the ability to shape light into solid structures.

Other questions surrounding light and mass have posed physicists problems throughout the last few centuries and continue to do so. For example, if light has no mass, how does radiation pressure exist? And why can't light escape from the gravitational pull of a black hole?

Anything Goes

Based on the new discoveries presented above, all bets are off. Now we know that light can become solid, and mass can travel through solid matter. What we once thought to be true is no longer so, opening up a new paradigm in which science can suggest ways a ghost can emit light, manifest from photons into solid forms, interact with the physical world around it, and still travel through walls. In the same way, I believe, aliens can take abductees through bedroom walls or the roof into a UFO. As the fictional character Sherlock Holmes famously uttered: "When you have eliminated the impossible, whatever remains, however improbably, must be the truth."

Sharing a Common Goal and Enthusiasm

The human desire to explore, combined with a thirst for knowledge and a hunger to learn, has driven man's basic instincts throughout history. Thus, both the paranormal investigator and ufologist share a common passion and drive to find answers and establish proof in their respective fields. Unfortunately, the majority of society does not wish to confront the questions posed by ghost and UFO sightings. Society does not want to remove itself from the safe paradigm it has adopted.

For years I have taken nonbelieving individuals on real-world investigations to prove ghosts exist. We would sit in a dark basement and witness a ghost walking through the room. We would engage in a long conversation via the ghost box—a device that creates white noise by scanning radio stations on a loop to generate disembodied voices. In many cases objects would move on command and high levels of EMF (electromagnetic fields) would be registered. At the end of such vigils the skeptic would often not change his or her mind despite all the visual and audio evidence to the contrary. I found this stubbornness to accept valid evidence to be very frustrating. For the believer, I have learned that no amount of evidence is necessary, and for the nonbeliever no amount of evidence is enough.

Society has castigated paranormal investigators and ufologists with humorous derision and mean-spirited contempt. I have personally experienced this with the press. During a paranormal investigation in Redwood Falls, Minnesota, I witnessed one of the most impressive UFO sightings of recent times. Five other investigators witnessed the three UFOs I recorded on twenty-five minutes of video. I also recorded empirical evidence on my equipment. Plainly we had experienced something real. The local newspaper ridiculed the sighting with a headline printed on September 23, 2017: "Ghost Investigator, Adrian Lee, Now Claiming UFO Sighting in Redwood Falls." I was not *claiming* it had taken place; clearly something had taken place. The newspaper chose not to print the photographs of the UFOs, which proved something actually had happened. The headline started with the term *Ghost Hunter*, which was irrelevant in this context and was employed only to get the reader's eyes rolling before the word UFO appeared.

Downplaying the significance of an event or emotion makes it easier for society to ignore an event; if you don't acknowledge it, you don't have to deal with it. This is why society often believes that obvious sightings and contacts are swamp gas, weather balloons, a trick of the light, or the strange imaginings of an eccentric.

John S. Carpenter, MSW, LCSW, outlines in *I Forgot what I Wasn't Supposed to Remember* why the majority of society struggles to acknowledge the presence of UFOs:

> Abduction by alien beings is hard enough for present day society to digest. In fact, many still doubt UFOs fly through our skies on a daily basis. We don't wish to believe in things unsettling, inexplicable, or beyond our control. Many who see strange things or have unexplained experiences just tuck them away— odd "quirks" or "weird" events. We then repress, or simply forget them as a matter of convenience.

Stephen Bassett is a political activist, commentator and columnist. He is a leading advocate for ending the prolonged government-imposed truth embargo regarding alien contact. In his essay "The (Exo)politics* of the contactee phenomena," he describes how abductees struggle with sharing their experiences due to the social stigma of abductions:

> Unknown thousands of human beings are involved. Often their entire lives have been shaped by their contact. Many are fully closeted about these experiences unable to tell even their own family members. Parents must deal with their children's involvement.

The Effect of Experiencing Both

The effect of seeing either a ghost or an alien can have a similar detrimental result on the experiencer. Ufologist and author November Hanson states this very simply in her book, *Mosaic of the Extraterrestrial Experience*:

> Seeing both changes people's lives.

Hanson continues to describe how society reacts negatively to an abductee's experiences:

> In the past a great deal of people kept their experience to themselves. They were smart enough to understand society and its ridicules of what is not understood.

Aliens and Ghosts as Demonic

Due to simple fear or religious beliefs, society classifies both UFOs and ghosts as evil and demonic. This gives a good reason to avoid the subjects and provides further ammunition to admonishers. Andrew Hennessey is a Scottish UFO experiencer and author of the book *The Turning of the Tide*. His work has been featured on the Discovery and History TV channels. In his article *Exopolitics? It needs to change*, Hennessey describes how aliens have demonic behavior projected onto them due to their behavior:

> Clearly, if you are a human who has been raped, abducted, grievously assaulted, harassed, had damage to property, unwanted medical research, implants, abortions, inflicted disabilities from beings that keep coming back despite repeatedly telling them not to—then, when you identify demonic behavior in your assailants—the very least you want to supply to the human rights court

is identifying information as to who the assailant was, e.g., a Caucasian, Asiatic, African, grey, tall, white, Anunnaki, etc.

He also describes the impact it has on a person's life:

Some who have a first encounter with nonhuman intelligent beings undergo a life change not dissimilar to the "near death."

A further example of how aliens appear to have no issue with inflicting physical harm is described by an anonymous author published in the *Journal for Abduction Research* entitled "One man's struggle for freedom from abduction has this abductee found a way to stop the aliens from taking him?":

Another thing began happening. I would wake in the morning and find one or both of my arms bruised. My arms had not been bruised when I'd gone to bed. Sometimes the bruising was minor; other times severe. Sometimes just one arm, sometimes both. Initially, I paid little attention to it. But then, while getting ready for work one morning, my wife asked, "What did you do to your arms?" I replied, "Nothing, why?" She replied, "Look at your arms!" I looked and said, "Damn! What happened?" This must be something I am doing to myself while I sleep, I thought. The arm bruising was so common I got used to seeing it. It was embarrassing, though, at work. People would ask, "What happened to your arms?" I started wearing long sleeved shirts even in warm weather.

I fought free of the strong grip of the Greys. This would happen when I glimpsed something I was scheduled for and wanted no part of it. Once

I became aware of how my arm received the
bruising, it immediately stopped. It's been more
than a year since I've had any bruising on my arms.
Truly, knowledge is power.

Elaine Douglass, MS, looks into the process of how aliens
break abductees in her essay "The breaking of Jim Sparks, or why
the aliens don't land on the White House lawn." Douglass describes
the psychological trauma inflicted by aliens:

> The psychological literature has a lot to say about the
> process of breaking people. In one book, *Battle for the
> Mind*, the author explains what has to be done to get
> an individual to "change long-standing beliefs, drop
> ordinary perspectives of common sense and become
> open to ways of thought quite foreign to the person's
> previous life." The first step, says the author, is to
> subject the individual to "intense trauma."

As well as physical and psychological abuses, aliens are also
capable of controlling the mind. Budd Hopkins is responsible for
bringing the UFO abduction phenomena to the attention of the
public and UFO community through his books. He has investigated
over seven-hundred cases and interviewed more than a thousand
witnesses over the last thirty years. In his essay "An Alien Agenda
Involving Hybrids," he states that aliens can manipulate and control
the brain, despite the stress and fear the abductees' experience:

> They are appalled, often repelled, and helpless, and it
> appears the whole thing is carried out through some
> control the aliens have over our neurological system.

A Fear of UFOs

UFOs and ghosts can elicit strong feelings of fear and terror, especially
in those not regularly exposed to them. We tend to fear what we don't

know. Barbara Lamb, MS, MFT, CHT, is a psychotherapist with experience in conducting regression therapy with abductees. Lamb describes how abductees emotionally respond to their abductors, as described in the *Journal of Abduction Encounter Research*, under the title "The Big Picture of Extraterrestrial Contact Experiences & How Regression Therapy Can Help":

> Regression therapy is the most helpful and effective way I know for getting to the source of a continuing problem, such as fear, trauma, confusion, or feeling victimized by an unknown source. After 15 years of conducting psychotherapy and seven conducting Regression Therapy, I discovered that the source of some people's distress or trauma is experiences they have had with extraterrestrial beings. These beings cause various responses in the people they contact—everything from wonder, awe, and enlightenment to extreme anxiety, fears and phobias, anger, resentment, and (rarely) the inability to function normally. Regression therapy and integration work can help people with any of these responses make sense of bizarre experiences and function better in their lives, even though the experiences may continue to happen to them.

Many abductees also experience positive encounters with well-meaning aliens. Dr. Richard J. Boylan, PhD, is a behavioral scientist, anthropologist, and certified clinical hypnotherapist. He provides hypnotherapy for clients to help them recall details of partially remembered encounters with aliens, stored in their unconscious memory. In his essay "Findings about the real Star Visitors versus the bogeymen of the cover-up's propaganda," Boylan reveals his belief that aliens are benign with positive qualities:

> I do not find credible reports of low-life aliens from these professionals, nor from the experiencers they

have worked with. On the contrary, the reports coming from behavioral science professionals describe intelligent, wise, compassionate, interested Star Visitors, who want what is best for our world and theirs.

I personally believe that good and bad aliens exist— as reflected within our own society when referring to humans. Unfortunately, humanity appears to be fulfilling the role of a laboratory animal for some of the more malevolent alien species.

A Fear of Ghosts

Ghosts can also elicit a feeling of fear and dread. An elderly Minnesotan resident once asked if I took a gun on paranormal investigations. I questioned how I would kill something that's already dead. He did not reply.

Investigator scratched at the Mounds Theatre in St. Paul, Minnesota.

Ghosts can exhibit harmful physical behavior and are capable of throwing objects and attacking individuals. I have witnessed ghosts scratching and pushing investigators. An example of a physical assault came in the basement of the Mounds Theater in St. Paul, Minnesota. An unseen hand grabbed a female investigator by the throat and threw her to the ground. We ascended to the sanctuary of the light and discovered fresh scratch marks across her back, as if somebody had brought the back of their hands together over her spine and clawed outward toward her hips. She could not have caused the scratches herself, and I cannot provide an explanation other than to label it paranormal.

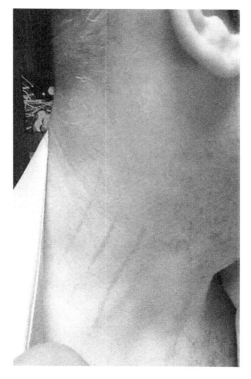

Scratched by an unseen hand in
Jackson, Minnesota.

When I visited a coffee shop in Jackson, Minnesota, I received my own personal experience of a ghostly scratch. The building was in the process of being remodeled, often a catalyst for paranormal activity. From the moment I entered the shop, the atmosphere felt angry and unhappy, as if charged with electricity. I did not feel my neck scratched, and it took a member of the staff to notify me of the visible marks. A claw mark went under my jaw in a downward motion leaving three red welts. A spirit was obviously unhappy with the process of renovation and was eager to catch my attention. I took a photograph on my phone to document the incident.

I also experienced a physical attack by a ghost at the Norshor Theatre in Duluth, Minnesota, in February 2018. Before the investigation, I was standing in the lobby checking my equipment. I felt a sensation on the back of my right hand and looked down to see a set of teeth marks in the skin. It looked like a child's bite; my hands naturally hang around the same height as a child. I documented the incident with several photographs. This did not feel like a malevolent action, and I believe the child was trying to gain my attention. I suspect every parent remembers their child going through a biting stage.

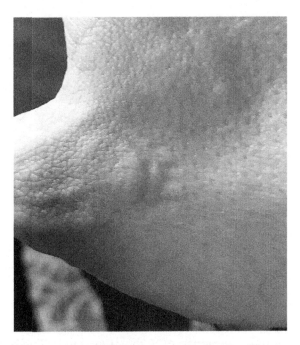

Bitten on the back of the hand at the Norshor Theatre
in Duluth, Minnesota.

The ability to throw objects around like a poltergeist would certainly allow spirits to aim missiles at unsuspecting investigators. During an investigation at Forepaughs Restaurant in St. Paul, Minnesota, I witnessed a fishing bobber thrown across the room. I had placed various spherical bobbers around the area and asked any listening spirits to pick one up. Almost instantaneously a bobber on a dining table launched itself across the room. It hit the wooden floor five feet away from its starting position, bouncing around the floor with a silence-shattering sound before rocking to a halt. I asked the spirit if it could knock over a second bobber to help prove its presence. This time a bobber I had placed on the newel post of a stairway could be heard bucking and bouncing down the steps in a journey that ended on the floor below.

I witnessed this phenomenon again at the Chase on the Lake Resort in Walker, Minnesota. I started the vigil that evening with the convention of sitting in silence. Suddenly, one of the larger bobbers I had positioned on the emergency push bar of the front double doors shot across the room and skipped over the floor like a stone skimming over a lake. It made a shattering noise that split the deathly quiet and made several of the team jump. Without missing a heartbeat, I leapt to my feet and ran to the rolling bobber, clutching my K2 EMF meter. As the bobber teetered to a standstill, I held the meter next to the trigger object and recorded a very high energy reading of twenty-five milligauss before the energy dissipated and disappeared.

Fears and Apprehension

As a paranormal investigator and ufologist, I can differentiate between ghost and UFO contact based on my own fears and apprehensions. For example, I could stand in a dark haunted basement and say, *here I am, come and talk to me.* I have seen death and I am alive, so I have an understanding of what a ghost is and what it once was. I would be more reluctant to stand under a dark sky in a field and say, *here I am, come and talk to me,* because whatever interacts with me will be beyond anything I can comprehend. I can understand and share a common humanity with a ghost; I cannot understand and share common humanity with a non-human entity.

It is possible to distinguish the ufologist and a paranormal investigator by the element of proactivity. The paranormal investigator can sit and wait for the ghostly entity to appear in the here and now. Poised with equipment at the ready, the investigation happens in the moment. Ufologists typically arrive after the event to conduct research retrospectively—unless the ufologist is standing in the middle of a field pointing a laser pen into the sky and feeling lucky. As previously stated, though, I would not be standing next to that ufologist.

Categorizing Hauntings

Hauntings can fall into two categories: residual hauntings and intelligent hauntings. A residual haunting appears in a certain place and time. It looks to the observer like a video of an event played back. No interaction can take place. An intelligent haunting is the product of a ghost or spirit that can interact with the observer and answer stimulus and response questions. The spirit has an awareness of itself and can act and behave independently of a set actions.

Regarding UFOs, anything that resembles a probe or scientific data collection device sent from a larger UFO cannot be interacted with beyond its prescribed mission and capabilities. Yet contact with aliens is shown to be possible in which dialogue is shared or instruction given. Thus, spirits and aliens can both operate as self-directed conscious beings or in a repetitive, programmed manner.

Things That are Probable

I now wish to introduce ideas that are statistically probable but lack definitive proof. In contemporary scientific thinking, the existence of alien life on other planets is statistically probable. In November 2013, research astronomers Erik Petigura and Andrew Howard, from the University of California, Berkeley, published details in the journal *PNAS* claiming one in five stars is like our own sun and hosts Earth-sized planets located within their *habitable zone*. They conservatively estimate that one in five stars could host habitable planets, from a galaxy of over one hundred billion stars, which provides the possibility of twenty billion planets.

Using data from NASA's Kepler space telescope, launched in 2009 for the purpose of finding earthlike worlds orbiting distant stars, Petigura and Howard are working on the premise that a perfect region and distance of a planet orbiting a star will allow water to stay in a liquid form on its surface, a factor believed to be essential to the creation of life.

In 1992, the first recorded planet outside of our own solar system was found orbiting a pulsar. Since this discovery, over one thousand exoplanets have been documented circling distant stars, and the number continues to grow exponentially. Astronomers can detect planets by the tiny dips in light as they pass in front of their stars, or through gravitational *tugs* on the star from an orbiting world.

The nearest exoplanet, roughly the size of Earth, is orbiting around Alpha Centauri at only four light years away, although it circles the star far closer than Mercury orbits our own sun. Our nearest Earth-sized exoplanet, with the possibility of supporting life as we know it, is only a mere twelve light years away.

To add to the number of planets capable of holding life, we must also expand our awareness of how many galaxies now actually exist that could host these planets. The MeerKAT radio telescope first became operational in July 2016 and provided some incredible images. The new telescope allows astronomers to look deeper into space than ever before. In a small region of sky previously believed to contain only seventy galaxies, it detected another 1,300. The phenomenal power of this instrument is yet to be unharnessed as it currently operates at a quarter of its full capacity, using only sixteen of an eventual sixty-four receptor dishes.

Once completed, the system will use the power of three thousand dishes from all over the world to peer into deep space. It's set to be one hundred times more sensitive than any current radio telescope. This incredibly powerful telescope will not only discover previously unknown galaxies, it will explore black holes and dark energy to trace the origins of the universe.

Two Trillion Galaxies

Scientists now believe the observable universe contains at least two trillion galaxies—twenty times more than previously thought. A British-led team of international astronomers came to this conclusion after converting images from the Hubble Space Telescope and observatories into three-dimensional maps. The research, co-funded by the Royal Astronomical Society, appeared in the *Astrophysical Journal* for October 2016.

The images allowed the scientists' calculations to define the density of galaxies as well as the volume of separate small regions of space. Astronomers had previously thought the observable universe contained around one hundred billion galaxies, but the new study suggested that many more galaxies had existed during earlier epochs of the universe's history. When it was only a few billion years old, ten times more galaxies had filled the universe than is the case today.

The total number of historic galaxies was expanded to an estimated two trillion. Lead scientist Professor Christopher Conselice from the University of Nottingham said:

> Finding more galaxies in the past implies that significant evolution must have occurred to reduce their number through extensive merging of systems. We are missing the vast majority of galaxies because they are very faint and far away. The number of galaxies in the universe is a fundamental question in astronomy, and it boggles the mind that over 90% of the galaxies in the cosmos are yet studied. Who knows what interesting properties we will find when we study these galaxies with the next generation of telescopes?

All of these findings prove that alien life is statistically probable. Over the course of the next year it is believed that NASA's Mars InSight lander will find life in microorganism form. At the end of 2018, Dr. Lewis Dartnell, who designed part of a rover that will be used to find signs of life on Mars, said there is a "very good chance" that it will happen. The professor and researcher at the University of Westminster said:

> What we don't know right now is if there is life on Mars and if there is—how similar is it to Earth? Is it really alien? Is it fundamentally different? Or does it just completely function in a different way? The sort of life we expect to find are single cells or hardy bacteria. That first kind of life is a microbial kind of life. What would excite me is to find something that had survived on Mars and bring it back to Earth to study and see how it works.

By examining and mapping the interior of Mars, scientists hope to learn how the rocky planets in our solar system turned out so different and why Earth became a haven for life. Dr. Dartnell designed the rover's Raman Spectrometer, an instrument capable of finding organic compounds. He explained:

> It is used on Earth to test the purity of drugs and explosives. It is really good at finding trace amounts of organic compounds, or signs of life.

The rover is a miniaturized laboratory that will drill two meters into the ground to search for bacteria, single-cell organisms and alien microbes.

Dr. Dartnell said:

> By drilling two meters underground we hope the soil has been protected from the harsh conditions on Mars, and we will find bacteria that can break down molecules. We will study the soil samples using different science experiments, and they will hopefully tell us a story. We are looking for the building blocks of life and to see if life on Mars has been there before. We want to look to see how warm and how wet it has been. It would be more great evidence that Mars was a warmer and wetter world and it was once like Earth.

In 2021, the European Space Agency (ESA) and the Russian Space Agency (RSA) will send the ExoMars rover to Mars. If life is discovered on our nearest planet in the near future, it would suggest that life is everywhere throughout the universe in abundance.

Shared Paranormal Phenomena

This chapter will examine commonalties based on witness reports and documented empirical data to establish that an overlap exists between aliens and spirits.

The Delivery of Messages and Information

Spirits and aliens both deliver messages and information. Perhaps the earliest documented way in which aliens have communicated with mankind is through crop circles. Crop circles are encrypted messages that require decoding to reveal the extraterrestrial information they contain. The first documented example of a strange crop formation dates from the 1678 pamphlet "The Mowing-Devil: Strange News of Hertfordshire." The British naturalist Robert Plot then reported strange rings of mushrooms in the 1686 publication *The Natural History of Stafford-Shire*. He proposed the movement of air as the cause for these strange formations.

A letter sent to the editor of *Nature* by amateur scientist John Rand Capron in 1880 also describes the sighting of crops flattened in a field but suggests they were caused by meteorological means. Then, in 1932, archeologist E.C. Curwen observed four dark rings in a field in Stoughton Down near Chichester, England:

> ...a circle in which the barley was 'lodged' or beaten down, while the interior was very slightly mounded up.

In the modern era, the National Security Agency (NSA) released documentation in 2012 that purported alien messages. Dr. Campaigne presented a series of twenty-nine messages received from extraterrestrial intelligences from outer space in the document "NSA Technical Journal Vol XIV No. 1" entitled, "Key to The Extraterrestrial Messages":

> Recently a series of radio messages was heard coming from outer space. The transmission was not continuous but cut by pauses into pieces which could be taken as units, for they were repeated over and over again. The pauses show here as punctuation. The various combinations have been represented by letters of the alphabet, so that the messages can be written down. Each message except the first is given here only once. The serial number of the messages has been supplied for each reference.

Aliens Provide Useful Information

Ufologist November Hanson revealed the results of a questionnaire completed by those claiming to be abductees in her book *Mosaic of the Extraterrestrial Experience*:

> Seventy-Five percent of the people asked if they felt the Greys were providing them with information that was useful said yes.

John Carpenter, MSW, LCSW, also stated in his essay "Which alien agenda is it?" that abductees receive messages and information from aliens:

> Abduction experiences sometimes include lectures, warnings, or holographic presentations about taking better care of our planet. Therefore, once the nuclear age began and pollution of our air and

environment became issues, UFO encounters and abductions seem to have increased significantly.

Dr. David M. Jacobs is an associate professor of history at Temple University in Philadelphia. He has been a UFO researcher for over forty years and conducted over one thousand hypnosis sessions with abductees. Jacobs, through his personal experiences and research with abductees, claims humans have completed tasks directed by messages from alien abductors. Jacobs documents his abduction experiences in the *Journal of Abduction Encounter Research* under the title "A Picture We May Not Wish to Gaze Upon":

> I began to hear disturbing accounts of other procedures that abductees had to perform but that seemed far more realistic than the rescue scenarios. An abductee will be told he or she has a specific job to do in the future. One of the most common jobs is crowd control. The abductee is to stand on a street and move people along—panicked humans, running and screaming. His job is to calm them, tell them it is okay, "everything is going to be all right, just move this way, keep moving, keep moving this way." I wrote about this in my book, *The Threat*, and I have had all sorts of accounts like this since.

Some messages from aliens seem intended to improve humankind. Stefano Breccia is an Italian ufologist with an engineering MA from Bologna University, Italy. In an essay entitled "Amicizia: a story of friendship in Italy," he claims aliens intend to do this by:

> …Elevating mankind, little by little, to a higher level of consciousness and morality.

In an article entitled "'Remembering' the Future? Something

New in Regression Results," ufologist and respected author Barbara
Lamb published evidence of aliens implanting knowledge about the
future into the mind of an abductee named Ken:

> This raised many questions for me. Was Ken once
> again being subjected to the external influence of
> the alien beings? For whatever reason, had they
> placed a dramatic scenario in Ken's mind and
> crafted it to look to him like a past event? Or, were
> we involved in a progression to a time in the future?
> I was familiar with progression. It is a method,
> induced through hypnosis, of attempting to acquire
> information about future events.

This work is informed by the theory that time may be
simultaneous, and if so it may be possible to see forward to events
that have not yet happened in our normal framework of linear time.

Spirits Delivering Messages

Spirits have been delivering messages within every culture for
millennia. We have already discussed the early writing of Pliny
the Younger and the paranormal phenomena of the Bible. The
play *Hamlet* by William Shakespeare and the tale of *A Christmas
Carol* by Charles Dickens both contain the delivery of messages
and information by ghosts as a central theme. I have personally
experienced spirits delivering messages and information throughout
my investigations via my psychic work and equipment.

A Dead Stable Worker Delivers a Message

During an investigation at the Chase on the Lake Resort in Walker,
Minnesota, I received a message from the spirit of a nineteenth
century stable worker. The contact took place in the basement's
mechanical room with several members of my team present.

I have found the ghost box to be a very valuable tool in making contact and having a dialogue with spirits. Ghost box devices scan radio frequencies at various speeds and can generate words and sentences believed to be from those in spirit. Sometimes called a *shack-hack,* these devices can be modified radios or purposely built devices for use in the paranormal field, such as the P-SB 7. Spirits can assemble the words presented to them on the radio to communicate in a way much like piecing together a ransom note with words taken from different newspaper headlines. Ghost boxes also generate white noise, allowing voices to be heard under the static. By recording these sessions with a DVR, I can listen retrospectively in a quiet and controlled environment. These tools are not a form of electronic Ouija board as the communication is via the device and not through me or any other individual. I simply turned on the device and began the conversation.

In this instance I asked who was with us, and the spirit clearly responded, "Edward."

"Hello, Edward," I said. I told him my middle name was Edward. "What year is it, Edward?" I asked.

"1905," he replied. In 1905, the site was home to the original Spencer Hotel and a lumberyard.

"Did you used to work here?"

"Yes," he replied.

I had not expected to engage with a worker from fifteen years before the speakeasy began operating. I asked if there was anything he wanted me to do.

His answer came back instantaneously. "Feed the horses!"

Horse feed or hay would have been difficult for us to access at short notice this time of night, but I did recall seeing a bowl of fruit in the lobby. "If I leave an apple, would that suffice—would that work?" I asked.

"Yes, an apple," Edward replied. "Thank you."

"Thank you for talking with us."

Apparently satisfied with the conversation, Edward retreated, and we had no further contact.

The Mechanical Room at the Chase on the Lake Resort
in Walker, Minnesota.

Ghost Warns of a Fire

The 1861 Maxfield House in Mankato, Minnesota is the oldest building left standing in the town. I investigated the property extensively in 2015 and 2016. During one of the basement vigils I conducted a very interesting conversation with a spirit called Charles who not only delivered information about his life but also issued a warning.

I turned off the lights, plunged the team into darkness and started the vigil. I wanted to know who was observing us, so I turned on the ghost box.

"What is your name?" I asked.

"Charles," a child said.

"Is your name Charles?" I asked for clarification.

"Danger!" The voice said loudly, then shouted to gain my attention. "Adrian!" He must have been listening when the group introduced itself at the beginning of the vigil.

"Why is there danger?" I asked.

"Death!"

"Why did you say death? Is there something I should be concerned about?"

Silence prevailed so I asked once more.

"Is your name Charles? Yes or no."

"Yes."

"Did you used to live here?" I continued.

"Yes."

"When were you here... a hundred years ago... ninety years ago?"

"Stop!" the voice shouted as I got to ninety. "You are a smart guy. Danger!" he shouted into the cold, damp darkness.

"Do you like us being here?"

"I can't breathe!" he exclaimed.

"Why can't you breathe?" I asked.

Remarkably, the spirit then asked me a question. This is a rare occurrence, and I do not recall many times when a spirit has taken the lead on a ghost box session.

"How did you get here?" he inquired. I now felt like I was intruding on his property.

"We were invited by the owner to talk with you," I said.

"We built the house," he replied.

"And it is a fabulous house," I stated.

"Exhausted," the voice said without me asking a question.

"Why do you hang around here?" I asked.

"Fire!" came the answer.

"When was the fire?"

No reply was forthcoming, so I asked, "Was it 1880... 1890... 1900...?"

He shouted "Yes" when I got to 1900.

"Nineteen hundred and what?"

"Four."

"Do you like what Jackie has done with the house?"

"Tired," he answered a second time. "Charles," he said once more.

We then experienced a long silence before I decided to finish the vigil.

"Will you say goodbye?" I asked.

"I'll say goodbye," a male voice replied.

I believe the 1904 fire was a traumatic experience for the family. Is it possible that an imprint of their emotional turmoil left an "intelligent residual" haunting like an imprint in time? I had never experienced such a phenomenon before.

During the next visit to the property I started a dialogue in the same location.

"Is Charles there?" I asked.

"Yes," came the reply in the now familiar child's voice. "I know you."

This indicated to me that the spirit had a sentient memory of my previous visit.

"Is your mother here?" I asked, wanting to confirm that Charles was the son of George Jr. and Bertha.

"Yes, I think so," he said.

I thought this to be a slightly odd reply in that he did not seem to know whether his mother was present or not. Perhaps he was unsure if his mother was with us in the room or back in the spirit realm where he had just come from. Then, without any prompting, the ghost box shouted out the name Bertha. This short, six-letter name instantly corroborated my historical research.

"What year was the fire? Nineteen what?" I asked.

"Four."

I knew the fire had happened in 1904, so once more I verified the research with the evidence I had received from the previous investigation.

The Basement of the Maxfield House.

Canby Theater Message

In Yellow Medicine County, Minnesota, a spirit named William wanted me to pass on a message to the new owners of the Canby Theater. I started a vigil in the basement below the lobby, and a spirit entered the room and registered on the EMF meter.

"Thank you for joining us," I said. "Did you work here?"

"No," came the reply in a very firm manner.

"Were you born in Canby?" I asked.

"No."

I deduced that this might be the spirit of a person who had built or owned the theater. "Did you own or build the theater?" I asked.

"Yes."

"What is your name?"

"Bill," he said in a loud and clear voice.

"Do you prefer Bill or William?"

"William," he responded.

This was vital evidence as a series of "yes" or "no" responses could be random. Yet here was a definitive answer to the question.

"Do you like how the restorations are going?" I continued.

"Yes!"

"Is there anything you would like to mention or bring up in terms of how the theater should be run?" I asked.

"Seven," came the mysterious response.

I did not understand this reply, but I made a note of his answer.

"Is there anything else you would like to say?" I asked.

"No, thank you," he said.

This seemed like a good time to end the dialogue, and I thanked him for his input.

When the teams reunited back in the lobby, I told the manager about the conversation that had taken place in the furnace room. I asked him if the mysterious response of "seven" had any significance. The manager told me that the board of the Canby Theater had met just days previously and discussed how much they should charge for admission when they reopened. They had settled on the sum of seven dollars. This would suggest that William had an awareness of those discussions and was in fact giving his approval to their decision.

The manager then informed me that one of the two brothers that built the theater was named William Flieder. The census record for 1940 lists William as being born in Minnesota on July 24, 1895. During this time he had been residing on Oscar Avenue in Canby with his wife Edna, thirteen years his junior. He died on February 1, 1983, at the age of eighty-seven.

The basement of Canby Theater in Canby, Minnesota.

Message at the Windom Theater

The theme of capitation and money-related issues also surfaced when I investigated the Windom Theater in Windom, Minnesota, in 2013 and 2014. The theater was built in 1914 and claims to be the oldest theater in Minnesota still showing films. I engaged in a dialogue with a spirit on the stage using the ghost box.

"Do you like being here?" I asked.

"Please help me!" a girl's voice said. "Help!" she said again.

"Why do you need help?" I asked.

"Adrian, you should know," she replied. This response indicated she knew who I was and understood what I knew based on my experiences with the theater.

"Hello," I said. "What is your name?"

"Hi," she replied, followed by "Lucy." This was a confirmation that I had received the right psychic information.

"Patience," she said.

"So is your name Patience?" I asked quizzically.

"No!" she said, allowing me to believe that the word patience was referring to the act of waiting diligently.

"Broke!" she said, directing the conversation.

"Do you not have any money?" I questioned.

"Yes," she responded. "Help me."

"Do you want some money?" I inquired. "Is that the reason you said 'help me'?"

"You are right."

"Money for whom?"

At that moment several strategically placed flashlights switched on and illuminated the vigil. I took this as a sign of encouragement.

"Tell me what you need, and I can help you," I said.

"Give me something!" she retorted.

"What?" I asked but did not receive a response. "Is the money for you?"

"Yes," she replied. "Thousands."

"What do you want the money for?"

"You are ignorant!" she replied bluntly and then quickly left.

I believed I knew what Lucy was asking for. The non-profit organization that ran the theater was under threat of having to close. Like many other small-town historic theaters, it was struggling to finance the hefty cost of a digital projector as film distributers moved to new technology. Raising funds was proving to be a difficult task. Lucy had expressed her concern because she would no longer have a stage to play.

I began working to raise an awareness of the theater's plight. I explained the situation on various radio shows and played the audio recording of the little ghost girl asking for money to keep her theater open. The recording of Lucy asking for money became a catalyst for donations. In some small way, then, she contributed in spirit to the theater staying open.

I arranged a follow-up investigation to ask Lucy what she thought of this success and the efforts of the theater board. I started the first vigil in the same place as before, behind the big screen on the stage. After turning on the ghost box, a presence appeared over my shoulder, and there was the same buzz and electricity I'd felt before.

"Would you like to say hi?" I asked, breaking the silence.

"Hi," Lucy said.

"Do you remember me?"

"Money," she said.

"Are you happy the money arrived?"

"Yes, yes!" She responded twice to reinforce the answer, followed by "Thank you!"

"You are welcome," I responded. "So you are happy it stayed open?"

"Yes!"

"Will you say goodbye?"

"Goodbye," she replied.

I received the information I was looking for and finished the vigil. Throughout my years of paranormal investigating I had never experienced a more remarkable and touching encounter.

The Windom State Theater auditorium, Minnesota

Messages Delivered Psychically

Messages have often been delivered to me and other paranormal investigators from the spirit world through the spoken word. Aliens also communicate messages and information to abductees, but usually through psychic means.

Abductees tend to use the word *telepathy* to describe alien communications. The *English Oxford Dictionary* defines the term telepathy as "the supposed communication of thoughts or ideas by means other than the known senses." The same dictionary describes the term psychic as "relating to or denoting faculties or phenomena that are apparently inexplicable by natural laws, especially involving telepathy or clairvoyance." *Clairvoyance* is the faculty of perceiving things or events in the future or beyond normal sensory contact. As previously shown, aliens have presented future events to abductees. So the terms *telepathy*, *psychic* and *clairvoyance* can describe the same experiences.

Bill Foster is an abductee and author of many non-fiction books including *The Black Triangle Abduction*. In his essay "The Greys want to know how we feel," he explains the alien's ability to read his thoughts instantaneously:

> In all other contact with the Greys my thoughts
> were comprehended and intercepted before I even
> finished formulating them to speak aloud.

Experienced ufologist and writer Stephen Barrett also believes aliens can deliver messages to mankind through telepathic means. He describes this phenomena in his essay "The (Exo)politics* of the contactee phenomena":

> Some contactees report receiving messages
> regarding pending catastrophic events and social
> breakdown. Some receive these messages in person
> while others receive them via a psychic process

without direct contact. US Government awareness of such events is sometimes implied.

Some claim to receive messages about a new era for the human race which includes assistance from off-world civilizations, participation in off-world political alliances, access to extraordinary new technology, travel to the stars, a world without war, enhanced mental powers, and more.

John Carpenter, MSW, LCSW, details in his article "Which alien agenda is it?" the way aliens use telepathy to communicate and the nature of their messages:

> Telepathic communications are usually to calm, persuade, or reassure. Most of the time the beings interact with the abductee in the same fashion as a nurse with a small child in a doctor's office: "Hold still… don't worry… this won't hurt… you'll be going home soon."

UFO researcher and abduction expert Elaine Douglass further highlights the extraterrestrial's use of telepathy on mankind in her essay "Is Bill Holden a free man?" Douglass discusses the experiences of abductee Bill Holden and the information he received through thought:

> Now, conversation, as far as that I'm going through is all telepathic and basically (this has happened to me twice now): Tell them to stop destroying Mother Earth. Tell them to learn to love one another.

Abductee Jayna Conkle documented her experience of alien communication via telepathy in an article in the *Journal of Abduction Encounter Research* entitled "These vermillion-skinned, high ranking alien females in shiny robes can turn invisible!" Conkle describes how orange female aliens communicated with her and fifty other women via telepathy:

It was a most peculiar sort of lecture, because it was utterly silent. I could hear the human women around me sighing softly, clearing their throats, and making the countless little incidental sounds people make, but the robed female Greys made no sound. Instead, the speech was communicated telepathically. The female making the speech was standing in front of a lectern, and the lectern seemed able to broadcast her telepathic communications to all the women in the audience simultaneously.

Telepathy Removes the Language Barrier

Mario Rangel is a leading Brazilian ufologist and hypnotist abduction investigator. He is the author of *Hypnosis in Ufology—in the USA, Brazil & elsewhere*. He documents the abductee's experiences of communication with aliens through telepathy undertaken in the experiencer's own language and geographically specific accent:

Using hypnosis I researched telepathy two times with complete success. I know telepathy is real and we can learn it. During abductions some persons think the ETs talked to them clearly in the abductee's language. During the investigations with hypnosis we cannot give any type of suggestion, and so when the abductee says the ET talked to him in good Portuguese, I ask, "Portuguese with a southern Brazilian accent, a northern Brazilian accent, an accent from Portugal, or how?" Generally the abductee thinks a little and remembers there was no sound and understands it was telepathy. If the abducted's eyes in this moment are open, it will be possible to see a curious movement inside which can be a register of a new information in his/her brain—it will be similar to saving information in a computer. As the abducted never before used telepathy, he or she thinks that because he understood perfectly the message it had to be in his or her language.

Alien's Use of Clairvoyance

November Hanson adds important detail to the process of alien telepathy in her book *Mosaic of the Extraterrestrial Experience*:

> We use the term telepathy. I do not care for that term, but I have not come up with a better one. Language is often a barrier when trying to convey meaning in this subject area. We are not talking about someone thinking a sentence, saying it out loud in their head and the words transmitted into someone else's mind. You would actually feel the communication. I would think there would have to be some kind of imagery associated with the communication to evoke feeling. Actually if imagery was used to imply meaning through telepathy that would make sense as you would not actually have to speak the same language.

Immense mental powers are required to undertake telepathy and to control the thoughts and actions of others. Dr. David Jacobs explains this theory and other mental abilities on his website:

> The aliens have immense powers of the mind. That is where they are most advanced, baffle many investigators and abductees, and cause doubt in the minds of people with no knowledge of aliens.

Neural trespassing is one of the intrusions we discussed earlier. In an article entitled "A Picture We May Not Wish to Gaze Upon," Jacobs describes the abductees' experience of what he calls a *mind-scan*:

Oftentimes I found these procedures were accompanied by a strange procedure in which an alien might stare into an abductee's eyes from a distance of a few inches away or closer. The abductee is unable to avert his or her gaze. They feel something happening inside of their minds. They "see" both static and flashing images. Emotions are generated of one sort or the other. Memories are looked at. A whole world of neurological patterns is happening in their minds while this kind of neural engagement is occurring.

Mind control and telepathy appear to be part of the same process. Budd Hopkins states in his text *An Alien Agenda Involving Hybrids* that hybrid aliens already live among us and are able to communicate through thought and the control of our minds:

As far as hybrids operating in the human world, we have many reports of them driving automobiles, shopping in stores, and behaving more or less naturally in other mundane places, but manifesting the kinds of powers aliens seem to have, i.e., the ability to control minds, and to communicate telepathically.

Telepathy and Contemporary Science

It may be possible to use technology to make us telepathic, which suggests that technologically advanced aliens could harness this method of communication. Published in the *Daily Mail* newspaper on April 8, 2012, a report highlighted the US Army's intention to create a helmet that allows soldiers to telepathically communicate with each other on the battlefield. The University of California-Irvine, in conjunction with labs in Philadelphia and Maryland, are undertaking a four-million-dollar research project. The Defense Advanced Research

Projects Agency DARPA was established in 1958 and is dedicated to expanding the Department of Defense's technology usage, some of which includes top secret research into the mind.

An example of this technology is the use of electrodes to pick up specific code words that individual soldiers are thinking. A computer recognizes those transmitted code words and registers the soldier's position. Specific messages relayed back to the soldiers indicate whether their progress toward the target is safe. So far 45 percent of the commands transmitted from one volunteer to another—such as "call in helicopter" or "enemy ahead"— have proven to be correct. That statistic is expected to improve with the development of the technology.

A physical attachment to the computer via electrodes or a technologically advanced helmet is required during these experiments. This allows the computer to interface with thoughts. Scientists are now considering how to sever that connection in a combat situation.

Telepathy Now

Research led by experts at Harvard University has shown that technology can now send simple mental messages from one person to another without any connection between the individuals. Neuroscientist Giulio Ruffini told the BBC's *Today* radio program on September 6, 2014:

> You can actually transmit information directly from one brain to another brain without intervention of the senses. The next step would be to try to find more powerful techniques to send more complex information.

What Can We Do About It?

If aliens can initiate mind control and telepathy in abductees what can we do about it? Michael Menkin has a degree in political science and over thirty years of experience in high technology and technical writing. He created a helmet he believes can block telepathic manipulation by aliens. He describes his invention in the essay "Report on alien abductions and the Thought Screen Helmet":

> The effectiveness of my invention, the Thought Screen Helmet, proves alien technology obeys physical laws. The Helmet uses Velostat, a carbonized plastic which blocks alien telepathic communication.

Spirits Using Telepathy

I have already documented examples in which spirits delivered verbal messages. When I work as a psychic, I receive messages and information for clients from their deceased relatives and loved ones via thought, the same process aliens prefer. The information I deliver to the client from the spirit is personal and detailed. This includes information I could not possibly know and which was often forgotten by the clients until I revealed it to them. Two memorable examples from my work illustrate this: the case of a deceased grandfather who reminded his adult granddaughter about the time capsule they had buried together in the corner of the barn; and a message delivered from a son to his mother thanking her for placing a toy train in his coffin. I have even helped spirits, through their own direction, by guiding cadaver dog units to their murdered missing bodies.

Psychic Messages Corroborated

In February 2018, I investigated the Duluth Depot and Railroad Museum in Minnesota. During a vigil in the textiles storage room, I psychically interacted with the spirit of an eight-year-old girl, Josie. She said her name was Jocelyn but preferred Josie. The room was originally the station master's office, and she described being lost and looking for her parents. She'd become separated from them in the bustle of the railway station. She presented herself to me psychically, and I saw her wearing clothing from the 1930s.

After conducting the psychic session, I turned on the ghost box to corroborate the psychic messages. I asked for the name of the spirit, and a young girl replied "Josie" clearly enough for all to hear. It was recorded on a DVR. I then asked how old she was and received the reply "eight." I then asked who she thought the president was, and she said "Roosevelt." Franklin D. Roosevelt was president from 1933-45. Josie's answers corroborated the information I had received psychically by placing her in that historical era.

Psychic Work in Long Prairie

The 1898 Kemp Opera House block is in Long Prairie, Minnesota. The basement was a typical period river rock construction. As soon as I began the session, I felt the presence of a dog. I even saw glimpses of its dark, shadowy form racing around at knee height. I wrote the name *Queenie* on my notepad and then felt the spirit of a woman arrive. Based on an earlier vigil on the top floor, I also thought a woman named Abby was in the building. I started to psychically ask this woman questions.

"What would you like to be called?"

"Bea," she responded.

"So you are Abby, but you would like to be called Bea?" I asked.

"Yes," she responded.

"How old are you?"

"Nineteen."

"Do you have any brothers and sisters?"

"Yes," she replied.

"Was 1934 the year of your death?"

"Yes," she responded again.

She then told me that her body had been stored in the building. I found this a remarkable statement. Who stores a body in an opera house? Bea explained that she had seen her own body laid out there as she looked on in spirit.

I then focused psychically on how Bea looked. She was a fresh-looking young woman with a jovial round face. Her hair, parted in the middle and pulled back into a bun, was mousey brown with some blondness in it. She was slender and wore a long, primrose-yellow dress with a high collar and a simple white pinafore. Although I collected the verbal information psychically, the rest of the team heard a faint female voice as she responded to my questions.

I wanted to verify the psychic work with other equipment so we would have two separate sources. I asked Scott to lead this session, and he turned on the P-SB 7 ghost box and started to ask Bea questions.

"Are you Bea?" he asked.

"Yes, yeah, yes." Her response was loud and clear.

Suddenly she called out, "Adrian!" I wondered if she was asking where I had gone now that Scott was leading the vigil.

"What is your age?" Scott asked.

"Nineteen."

"Is it easy for you to communicate with us?"

"Yes," she said.

"Were you born in Long Prairie?"

"Yes."

"What color is your dress?"

"Yellow," she said.

During our psychic interaction earlier, Bea had made me aware that she played a musical instrument, but I had not informed the team about that. Now I instructed Scott to ask what musical instrument she played, and he did.

"Violin," she responded.

I had previously written this information on my notepad. Her verbal response was valuable corroboration.

"Do you have a pet?" Scott asked.

"Dog," she said.

"What is the name of your dog?"

"Queenie."

Queenie was the name of the dog I had seen at the beginning of the vigil. The psychic information delivered by Bea had now been confirmed verbally by the equipment. Scott asked if Bea would say goodbye to us.

"Goodbye," she said.

Team member and local resident Lorna later researched the property at the Todd County Historical Society. She discovered in an old newspaper article that undertakers used the building from 1933 to the early 1940s. This historical information was previously unknown and only brought to light through our interaction with Bea and our investigation.

Messages about the Future

Psychics can predict the future based on messages received from the spirit world. Where these messages come from depend on the beliefs of the individuals receiving the messages. They come from spirits, spirit guides, guardian angels or the divine. Aliens also implant knowledge of the future based on alien abduction reports. Author Barbara Lamb documented how a regressed abductee named Ken received messages and information about the future from aliens. In an article entitled "Remembering the Future? Something New in Regression Results," she wrote:

> The being made Ken understand he was preparing Ken for this trip to Ohio and for being taken away from earth. The being showed him holographic scenes of earth quakes, violent storms, huge areas of earth flooded with water, dark clouds, black sky, and major upheavals which he said would soon take place on earth. Ken had heard about holograms of earth disasters that had been shown to other

abductees, and it therefore did not surprise him to be shown such holograms himself. Somehow it seemed natural to Ken the being would want to save him from the forthcoming disasters on earth.

Dr. Richard J. Boylan is a certified clinical hypnotherapist. Boylan specializes in regressing abductees through hypnotherapy to access subconscious details of their experiences. Through his work, Boylan believes aliens are implanting messages to educate and warn mankind about the future. He presented his conclusions in the essay "Findings about the real Star Visitors versus the bogeymen of the cover-up's propaganda":

> The Star Visitors' messages contain warnings for us of dangers we are presenting to ourselves by our ecological, military, social and economic behaviors. They provide us with important and useful information for advancing our society and ourselves mentally and spiritually. The Visitors are preparing us (via messages relayed through select human experiencers) to socially accept the reality of extraterrestrial contact and are readying us for joining the larger community of inhabited worlds.

Some Star Visitor races are here to teach, some to guide, some to heal, some to advance us culturally, some to advance us biologically, some to study us, some to passively observe, some to take samples of our flora and fauna, and some to stand guard to protect us or to protect space from our plutonium-contaminated space probes and space weapons systems. None are here to invade—none.

Aliens Bestow Psychic Skills to Abductees

Farah Yurdozu is a Turkish UFO researcher, writer and psychic, with a specialty in abductions and close encounters. In her essay "Jinn or ET? Three Generations of a Turkish Family's Paranormal

Experiences," she explored the claim that three generations of her family had the ability bestowed upon them by aliens to see ghosts and be psychic:

> After a while they noticed their five-year-old son was able to see ghosts. Wherever he went he saw beings, heard voices, communicated with people only he could see. The other children also suddenly developed psychic abilities. For instance, one of the daughters, my grandmother, became a capable psychic medium. All her life she dealt with ghosts, apparitions and spiritual contact just like her sisters and brothers.

My grandmother and her siblings were the first generation of psychics in our family. Something made them psychic. Something was given to my family which opened their spiritual "third eye" to the unknown. When the Reptilian visitors said, "From you to three generations...," did they mean these psychic powers?

Elaine Douglass states that Joe Montaldo, the head of the International Center for Abduction Research (ICAR), will not consider an abductee's account unless they consider themselves to be psychic. Douglass explains this in her essay "The Connor O'Ryan story: Was this S-4 whistleblower given a fatal disease by the US government?"

Joe Montaldo, the head of ICAR, deals with a lot of abduction cases. Joe says when someone presents themselves as an abductee or a possible, "If they're not psychic, we don't even consider the case."

Aliens either believe it is easier to communicate with abductees if they have a latent psychic skill or they make the abductee psychic in order to communicate.

Aliens Create Psychics

Eve F. Lorgen, MA, described a more clandestine reason for implanting psychic skills into abductees. Lorgen has conducted research and counseling in the alien abduction field for over twenty years. She has degrees in Biochemistry and Counseling Psychology. In her article "Scavengers of Passion," she describes aliens giving psychic abilities to abducted partners, allowing them to feel, sense, and communicate with each other in the psychic realm for the purpose of harvesting their energy:

> The instigators of the love obsession now set off a series of emotional highs and lows with accompanying paranormal features, such as spontaneous remote viewing of the targeted partner, empathic and telepathic connections, telesthesia, and out-of-body, "astral" visitations with the mate. (Telesthesia can be described as the perception of the energy field of another individual from whom you are separated by many miles.) Bizarre synchronicities regarding the targeted partner occur repeatedly in such a way as to maximize the need to be with the lover, fueling the obsession.

I believe you can teach individuals to be psychic, a skill we all have dormant inside us. Who has not randomly thought of someone, only to receive a text or phone call from that individual seconds later. Who has not experienced a sense of foreboding, only to discover later that a loved one has been involved in some kind of trauma or tragedy? While driving, you may have felt confused about the directions to your destination but suddenly felt drawn to a particular route only to find out it was the correct one. When house-hunting, you may have found yourself attracted to a particular house while walking up to it or have taken an instant dislike to one without even venturing inside. At these moments we are listening to our psychic minds. These events happen sporadically throughout our lifetimes. As a psychic, they could happen to me every minute of every day if I so chose. Everyone can achieve psychic skills.

I am therefore not surprised that aliens choose to embrace this form of communication, as it removes barriers. If the abductee and alien are not physically in the same location, they can still communicate. This is how I communicate with spirits. The barrier of language between the alien and the abductee is also removed when communicating psychically. I do not need to know Spanish if a Spaniard is psychically sending me the image of a cat.

I teach psychic development classes. It would appear from the abductee accounts that aliens have found ways to speed up this process, perhaps by accessing parts of the brain that allow these skills to work. Or maybe they have mastered the technology we are just now developing to facilitate psychic communication.

Visited in Dreams

Within the metaphysical world, spirits visit us in dreams. These dreams normally involve a deceased loved one arriving in spirit to deliver healing, messages, or comfort. A visiting spirit can be any individual we once knew or have yet to meet who wants our attention. Spirits can appear full-bodied or reveal just their faces. Messages tend to be applicable to one's current life and situations and are typically delivered verbally or through imagery.

Aliens and spirits are more likely to contact us during sleep, as our defenses are down and there are fewer distractions such as watching television, listening to the radio, family members intruding, or waking thoughts. Such distractions can prevent us from sensing, seeing, hearing, and feeling the subtle energy of those in spirit. During sleep we also release our boundaries from fear, doubt, and questions. Abductees have spoken of how aliens can access dreams to communicate messages.

Debra Patella began to experience extraterrestrial interactions during her sleep and describes this phenomenon in her essay "A Not-so-Ordinary Experience" published in the *Journal for Abduction Research*:

The word "experience" I apply only to what happened that night and since, because for more than 25 years previously I had considered all my memories of ETs and UFOs to be merely dreams, not experiences. They happened after I fell asleep, at night, in my dreamtime. In the morning, I always felt relieved and laughed at the crazy dreams of the nights before.

Patella believes we can access places and people in spirit during our sleep:

Could these experiences be happening in another dimension and only appear to be a dream or a nightmare? Do we leave our bodies and astral project to these other places? Do our spirits walk in these strange and unusual places, then return to our bodies at dawn? Do we visit our friends out of state and our ET friends in their ships and in other galaxies during the night, waking up the next passing off our limited recall as only a silly dream?

Reports also suggest an abductee can have his or her spirit removed during sleep for the alien's own needs. Elaine Douglass documents her work with an abductee called Jim in an article entitled "The breaking of Jim Sparks, or why the aliens don't land on the White House lawn." She describes how aliens took Jim in his sleep:

That year, for almost a year, Jim had dreams of being walked out of his house during the night. Abruptly, though, the modus-operandi changed, and he begins to be taken in a violent and terrifying manner. Later Jim will be extremely grateful to the aliens for those occasions when he is not taken in a terrifying manner.

To physically remove an abductee during sleep would suggest that an unknown alien science or a paranormal phenomenon was used to remotely locate the sleeping individual and remove the body from a bed into a UFO through the physical barriers of walls and roofs. I have read many accounts of abductees declaring they could not avoid abduction during sleep, even if they hid in motels, cars, or other random locations.

Aliens and Previous Lives

Memories and experiences from another era can influence a current way of being. Hypnotherapy can regress individuals to previous periods in their lifetimes. Hypnotherapy can also be undertaken when interviewing abductees to recall abduction details. Barbara Lamb, MS, MFT, CHT, is a licensed marriage and family therapist, certified hypnotherapist and regression therapist. In her article "The Big Picture of Extraterrestrial Contact Experiences & how Regression Therapy Can Help," she documents how clients believe aliens have contacted them before this lifetime:

> When experiencers ask why they, in particular, have been selected to be visited, they are often shown that during a spiritual state before coming into this lifetime, they made agreements with the Extraterrestrials to cooperate with them during this life. Or, they are shown they were once members of that group of beings during a previous lifetime, are currently one of their representatives here on earth, and have agreed to be studied by the beings to further understanding of the human race and life on earth.

From the types of messages delivered, the commanding of tasks, and information relating to the future, the modus operandi of spirits and aliens when communicating is remarkable. The delivery of messages can take place through psychic means, dreams, and even past life experiences. Advanced alien races may have investigated how ghosts and spirits have communicated with the living and used that information to develop technology to replicate the processes. These studies may allow them to stimulate the parts of the brain that allow psychic communication. A biomimicry study of the spirit world for an alien race's own benefit may not be that farfetched when we examine the similarities.

How Ghosts and UFOs Travel

Various theories have been proposed within the UFO community to address a major problem of intergalactic travel: how to bridge the vastness of space to visit other worlds. Current technology cannot generate the speeds required to access the universe; our nearest star is Alpha Centauri 4.37 light years away.

The fastest humans on record were the astronauts of the Apollo missions. During a return from the moon in 1969, the capsule of Apollo 11 reached a peak speed of 24,790 mph. NASA's current Orion spacecraft will carry astronauts into a low Earth orbit and eventually break this record. Its first crewed mission will be in 2021 with a planned flyby of an asteroid captured in lunar orbit followed by a months-long mission to Mars. But even Orion technology remains much too slow to explore the universe.

Speed is Not the Problem

Speed, defined as a rate of motion, is not a problem for us physically as long as the speed is relatively constant and in one direction. Humans should be able to travel at rates just short of the speed of light under those conditions. But our fragile, water-based bodies will have to contend with significant new hazards that come with high-speed travel. Acceleration and deceleration could be lethal.

If we travel at speeds close to the speed of light, we will have to accelerate and decelerate patiently. The physical trauma of a car crash shows the destruction caused to the human body when it travels from a mere tens of miles per hour to zero in the span of seconds. The destruction is the result of inertia. Any object with mass resists change to its state of motion as shown in Newton's first law of motion: "an object at rest stays at rest, and an object in motion stays in motion with the same speed and in the same direction unless acted upon by an outside force."

In early aviation, pilots reported strange symptoms related to speed and directional changes. These included temporary vision loss and a sensation of leadenness or weightlessness in the limbs and body. These sensations were gravitational forces or G-forces, units of accelerative force upon a mass such as a human body. One G is equal to the pull of Earth's gravity toward the planet's center at 9.8 meters per second squared.

Other Dangers of High-Speed Space Travel

At velocities close to and beyond the speed of light, stray hydrogen gas atoms, pieces of space debris, and micrometeoroids become high-powered bullets exploding into a craft's hull. The cosmos's ambient hydrogen would become a bombardment of intense radiation; the hydrogen would shatter into subatomic particles and pass into the ship, irradiating both the crew and equipment. At around 95 percent the speed of light, the hydrogen exposure would result in instant death. The craft would also heat up to temperatures that would melt any known material; all water-based human crew would boil.

Traveling at the speed of light may not be beyond the technology of aliens, but the erratic high-speed maneuvers and right-angled turns of UFO sightings suggest that G-forces do not affect the alien passengers, or perhaps the extraterrestrial travelers have found a way to negate it. Other concepts, then, are required to explain how intergalactic travel might be possible. The book *Extraterrestrial Odyssey* by William McNeff, Craig R. Lang, and Roger Kvande highlights the problem:

> One of the arguments used to claim that extra-
> terrestrial aliens cannot travel to earth is that the

distances are too vast, therefore space travel would
take long (longer than the lifetime of the creatures
aboard the craft) and the energy requirements
would be so great as to make interstellar journeys
impractical. But if there were some way to "jump
around" space-time at widely separated points it
would become feasible.

Witness descriptions of how some UFOs move support the
theory that extraterrestrial vehicles can suddenly appear in one part
of the sky and then suddenly disappear and reappear in another.
To the eye, this looks like an erratic zigzag movement because the
journey between each position is undetectable. A benchmark used
for calling a light in the sky a UFO (rather than a satellite or plane)
is its display of an erratic flight pattern characterized by sharp-
angled turns and the ability to jump from one place to the next. This
behavior is common in the MUFON archives.

The Tehran Dogfight

One of the most famous cases of UFO contact with an erratic
vehicle flight pattern remains one of the most impressive military
encounters ever recorded. It is documented in a four-page US
Defense Intelligence Agency DIA report. The "Tehran dogfight,"
as it was called, took place on September 19, 1976, after radar
and visual sightings confirmed a UFO over the Iranian capital of
Tehran. The Imperial Iranian Air Force command post at Tehran
also obtained four eyewitness reports of the incident from civilians
on the ground. The witnesses described an object similar to a star
but much brighter. Two F-4 Phantom II jet interceptors from the
Shahrokhi Air Force Base in Hamadan scrambled to intercept.

When the first aircraft approached within twenty-five
nautical miles of the object, the jet lost all instrumentation and
communication capabilities. When the pilot broke off the intended
intercept, all systems resumed functioning. The second jet locked

its radar onto the object at a range of twenty-seven miles. The radar signature indicated the UFO was the size of a Boeing 707. When the jet closed in the object began to move, keeping a steady distance of twenty-five miles from the F-4. The intense and brilliant lights of the object alternated between blue, green, red and orange, flashing in sequence rapidly in a square pattern.

While the object and the F-4 continued on a southerly path, a smaller second object detached itself from the first UFO and advanced on the second F-4 at high speed. Believing he was under attack, the Iranian pilot tried to launch an AIM-9 sidewinder missile, but he lost all instrumentation, including his weapons control systems and communication. He took evasive action, and the second UFO object fell in behind him at three to four miles away. It then turned and rejoined the primary UFO. The lost instrumentation of the F-4 resumed functioning as the jet turned away from the UFO.

The crew of the second F-4 then observed another brightly lit object detach itself from the other side of the UFO and drop at a high speed. The crew expected it to strike the ground and explode, but it landed gently. The crew overflew the site at a lower altitude and marked the position of the touchdown. The crew then sighted another object farther away—a cylinder-shaped vehicle with bright, steady lights on each end and a flashing light in the middle. The object overflew the F-4, nearly causing a collision.

The pilot of the first F-4 estimated that the UFO was traveling between two and three thousand miles per hour. He claimed the object was beyond the speed and power of his own craft. The second F-4 pilot said the main object emitted four objects: one that headed toward him and later returned to the main object; one that he unsuccessfully tried to fire upon; another that followed him back; and one that landed on the desert floor and glowed. His copilot gained a close sighting of the UFO that had directly approached. He described it as a round plate or saucer with a canopy or cockpit that looked like a half-ball bathed in a dim orange or yellowish light. He could not see the crew. He said the UFO displayed an inordinate degree of maneuverability.

Erratic UFO in Belgium

Another incident involving erratic and angular UFO movements occurred in the Wallonia region of Belgium on March 30, 1990, also prompting a military interception. Thousands of people reported seeing an aircraft exhibiting uncharacteristic flight patterns. Citizens and public officials, including police officers and air traffic controllers, described a large, triangular object capable of low-altitude flying and slow hovering with erratic high speeds and acceleration. A radar observation at Eupen in Belgium also reported the UFO in their airspace, and several other ground-based radars obtained signals from the same object at the same time. Reports continued into the early morning of the next day. Two F-16 fighter aircraft of the Belgian Air Force attempted to engage with the unidentified aircraft, but poor visibility that evening prevented the pilots from seeing the object. This sighting represents one incident from an extensive period of UFO activity over Belgium and its neighboring countries that year.

Bizarre UFO Movement in Eveleth

On June 20, 2008, three witnesses observed a UFO for thirty minutes between eleven and eleven thirty p.m. from the yard of their home in Eveleth, Minnesota. The daughter first noticed a light in the sky due to its erratic movements. She notified her mother and her son's friend to come outside to observe the strange object. All three claimed it looked far away, like a star, but it blinked regularly, changed color, and would flash occasionally from its sides. Its irregular movements were sometimes slow and at other times fast, but all were contained in a small general area. All three observers agreed that the object could not have been a plane, helicopter, or satellite because of its unusual movements.

Virginia UFO Sighting

Ken Pfeifer of MUFON New Jersey received a report regarding a UFO flying in an erratic manner on April 14, 2011, in Herndon, Virginia. Two low-flying military jets attempting to intercept the object caused the foundations and windows to rattle in the houses of Herndon. The disturbed witnesses came out of their homes and saw an erratic, fast-moving, star-sized object. The UFO made no sound as it escaped the jets by using an evasive, darting, and sometimes circling flight pattern. A twenty-year-old male eyewitness described the object as having a fast-repeating pattern of three pulsing blue and white lights followed by a quick single flash. The jets flew within the vicinity of the sighted craft for a second pass, but the object easily eluded the military jets. The object then disappeared out of sight. Two additional witnesses from the same area also reported the UFO.

This area of Herndon is a no-fly zone for small aircraft as it is only twenty miles west of Washington, DC. It is the airspace for the final approach of Dulles Airport, and any military aircraft in this part of the sky would only be there for interventional purposes.

UFOs Appearing and Disappearing

Three witnesses observed a triangular UFO on June 25, 2014, in Lakewood, Ohio. The object had an erratic flight pattern and appeared at times to cloak itself and disappear. The following statement from MUFON case 57384 is from a witness to the event:

> My friend's wife all of a sudden said, "What's that?" I looked up and saw an object with three lights start to dim, and it looked like it started to cloak…

> It had this weird aura around it, and it looked kind of like it was surrounded by water and it started to disappear. I could see what looked like a black

craft, but it happened so fast that I can't say for
sure what color it was.

The wife of the witness's friend had a second experience:

She saw three bright, reddish-orange lights in the
formation of a triangle in between the trees, and
then she followed it until it went behind their
house. She said she saw the same weird 'cloaking'
effect that I saw.

The witness said he felt odd just before and just after the event:

I remember feeling a very weird sensation in my
body right before she said, "What's that?" I of
course had some anxiety afterwards, but the feeling
I had right before I saw it was different.

The state of Ohio recorded twenty-six UFO reports for the
month of May 2014.

Bloomington UFO

In September 16, 2012, a witness saw a UFO suddenly disappear
in Bloomington, Illinois. She and her husband observed a skinny
cigar-shaped object and reported the encounter to MUFON. They
were driving in the country when they witnessed the object. They
had both lived in the area for over thirty years and were familiar
with the local aircraft:

We were on our way home driving west on Route
150. We had just left the Freedom Gas Station
on the corner of Towanda/Barnes Road and 150.
I glanced at the time on the car clock, and it was
10:38 a.m.

The woman recognized the object had no wings:

I am just trying to figure out why I can't see the wing and what type of new plane it is. It was so skinny, oblong and reflective. Then I determine that we are almost parallel, and I must not be able to see the wing because it's just blending with the side of the body of the plane, since we were both not quite level with one another.

The witness was able to see the object more clearly:

Then I noticed that the top extending back is a brilliant, reflective silver and the bottom from the middle of the craft to the front of the craft is black. Like two entirely different materials. In the middle where the two metals meet, but more on the silver side, is small, rectangular-like, black squares (not windows) horizontally in a line. I notice these because I'm intent on looking for a wing.

The witness also noticed the object appeared to be stationary and hovering:

It's still just sitting. It's not banking or turning, not descending, and we are starting to kind of pull ahead of it, which I thought was strange. At this point is where I start to question, what am I seeing?

The woman looked away briefly from the object to talk with her husband. When she turned back the object had gone:

I turned my head long enough to say, "Of course I'm listening," and immediately I look back out my window. Gone. I had only looked away mere seconds, and it was gone. Completely gone. No vapor trail, no... nothing. I looked up through our sun roof, took off my seat belt and turned to look out the back windows—the rear windows. It's nowhere. It just disappeared.

The witnesses reported a power drain on a cell phone during the encounter.

Zigzagging UFO

I personally interviewed an eyewitness in 2016 who saw a UFO moving erratically. Misti is a professional, working mother of three living in Mankato, Minnesota. At the beginning of 2005, she was driving at night with her sister on Highway 212 in Eden Prairie, Minnesota. Suddenly a round, bright, white light appeared out of nowhere and zigzagged through the night sky in an easterly direction. Through the windscreen of the car they witnessed the UFO move quickly back and forth four times before disappearing. Both witnesses expressed fear and bewilderment.

Disappearing and Transforming UFO in Willmar

At seven p.m. on August 31, 2012, I witnessed an erratically moving, appearing-and-disappearing UFO. I was driving south at sixty-five mph on Interstate 71 in Minnesota from Belgrade to Willmar. The sky was clear with no wind and excellent visibility. I entered the two-lane bypass road that runs south of Willmar to Olivia and noticed two tall wind turbines on my left. Suddenly I saw a large, azure-blue sphere in the space between the two wind turbines. It hovered approximately halfway between the ground and where the bottom of each blade passes in front of the tower. I estimated this to be an altitude of 130 feet.

I slowed down as I approached the part of the road that goes within one hundred yards of the turbines. The sphere started to move slowly to the left toward the first tower and then disappeared. Seconds later it reappeared in the position I would have expected had I witnessed the whole journey. It then traveled slowly in front of the first turbine tower. The left and right sides of the sphere appeared wider than the tower's width of twenty-two feet. Based on this visual evidence I now estimate the sphere to be roughly twenty-eight feet in diameter.

The sphere disappeared for a second time and reappeared moments later on the same trajectory. Again its trajectory between these two points was invisible. The object continued its travel from right to left and then disappeared for a third time. This time it reappeared as a cigar shape in the same color but with black tips at each end. The sudden transformation startled me. Suddenly it flew at great speed at a forty-five-degree angle into a thick copse of trees fifty yards from the turbines. The whole encounter lasted fifteen seconds.

Accompanied by the State Director of MUFON Minnesota, Lorna Hunter, I went back to the site the following day to investigate the wooded area. We scoured the dense undergrowth but found no traceable evidence.

An artist's impression of the Willmar UFO incident.

A Body of Evidence

I have begun to piece together multiple competent eyewitness accounts from various locations using both primary and secondary sources. These accounts involve radar detection, pilot contact, electrical failures, erratic maneuvering, angular turns at high speed, and no visible journeys between sighting points of each object.

The evidence suggests that UFOs use the practice of collective thought. This concept proposes that when aliens think they want to be somewhere, they can suddenly be there. The sudden appearance and disappearance of sighted crafts support this theory. If I ask you to imagine being at your local grocery store and you immediately imagine being there, you do not also imagine the journey that takes you to the store. Evidence supplied by abductees and experiencers supports the theory that thought can be a mode of transport.

Piloting a UFO with Thought

On December 19, 2017, the British press reported the story of Mr. Miller, an alleged former Area 51 employee who claimed to have piloted a UFO with the power of thought. Mr. Miller revealed that hidden inside the Groom Lake facility are aliens, spacecraft, and evidence of extraterrestrial life. He even claimed to have test-piloted one of the alien flying vehicles:

> I do remember they brought me inside the craft and up to the pilot's seat. There was only room for one person in the giant craft. I looked around the cockpit and only saw a seat. No joystick, no steering wheel, no other controls. There was, however, a helmet. They told me the craft was controlled telepathically. I was told to imagine the craft starting to float off the ground, but it didn't work. Instead I had to imagine that I was the craft, like part of it, and I began thinking of myself floating off the ground and I felt the vibrations.

Mr. Miller suggested he may have experienced time-travel after blacking out during the experience:

> I was 500 feet off the ground, then the vibrations of the engine stopped. There was no ejection button on the craft. I was effectively helpless. The craft was plunging towards the ground and I went unconscious. The next thing I knew I was in the hospital. A man in a black suit came in and explained to me what happened. He said right before the craft hit the ground, it just went boom, disappeared. Then in the middle of the night, they heard a loud crashing noise outside. The craft had crashed in the same spot. The scientists hypothesized that the craft had time-traveled.

Thinking Your Way to Mars

An abductee describes piloting an alien craft to the surface of Mars in the book *Extraterrestrial Odyssey* by William McNeff and Craig R. Lang. The UFO asked the abductee to reach out and imagine grabbing the planet through a thought as described here:

> It appears that a virtual mind-meld happened when RK was inside the ship in the proper position, and by merely thinking of "grabbing" the planet, he induced the ship's mind/computer to generate an attractive force between the ship and the planet. The ship had no verbal language; it communicated with me by sending experiences, pictures and concepts.

It is, of course, difficult to reach out and grab something you have no knowledge or understanding of. The boy knew of the existence of Mars without having any in-depth experience of the planet, but the vehicle completed the action after RK placed the intention.

UFO Controlled by Thought

In *The Alien Abduction Files: The Most Startling Cases of Human Alien Contact Ever Reported*, by Kathleen Marden and Denise Stoner, an abductee explained that UFOs are controlled with thought and through using the mind:

> Experiencers are now stating that they are being trained to operate the craft by using their minds to control it.
>
> She and several other experiencers had independently informed Marden they believed the craft was in part biological—this allowed for the craft to receive the thought. Kathleen Marden interviewed abductee Denise Stoner who describes a central core that controls the craft:

> STONER: He takes me into a room. It's connected to the center of the craft and the outer rim. It has its own atmosphere.
>
> MARDEN: The room has its own atmosphere?
>
> STONER: Yes.
>
> MARDEN: What does it feel like?
>
> STONER: I stepped into this room, and there was a total change in the atmosphere. And it's slightly… It feels like it wants to spin, but it's not.
>
> MARDEN: What do you see in the room?
>
> STONER: Its blackness and its cold. But I don't believe that it's solid. It's so black. There's a pole, and in the center of the pole there's a device… mechanical, and there is something wrapped

around it. Then there are two arms that come out, and they vaguely resemble the accordion tubing from a dryer... maybe. And they come out from that and then go down to a flat plate. But then it's the interior that's alive. You just know that it's alive, and the whole thing inside that center block is in motion. It can think. It operates the craft. It runs the craft.

MARDEN: Where did you see this? Was that in the examining room that you were in? (Again I attempt to lead Denise to tell me it was in the examining room in order to test her.)

STONER: No. He took me out further down the hall, and he said, "I'm going to show you the center of the craft. It's capable of shielding itself... of protecting itself... of passing through anything that flying through space can toss at it. It can pass through time... time. It could not do this until a few years ago." This is something they just, in their time, recently developed. It's not... I'm not feeling the fear, but at the time it was very frightening.

MARDEN: Did you express fear at that time?

STONER: Yes.

MARDEN: Did he respond to that?

STONER: He said I would never be able to understand the enormity of what he was showing me. This entity brought them here in it. This biological machine brought them here in it. I asked if there was a console and a point of operation. Did he have to operate this from any point in this thing? I didn't have a word for it. I felt disoriented. The room makes you feel disoriented. And he said,

"Not any longer. It is a thought process. And that is new also. And now we must take you back. Oh, it's affecting your muscles." He said I must leave. (Denise's body start to jump around and her limbs thrash about as if she is being hit by pulse waves.)

MARDEN: You can relax now. Your muscles won't jump anymore. You can leave. You're getting out of there... getting out of there. You're calming down. You're calming down. You're calming down. You're very relaxed now... very very relaxed. Your muscles will no longer jump. Take a deep breath in and release it. You're very calm... very calm and collected. Your muscles won't jump anymore. (Denise calms down.) Now think about the time that your muscles jumped. Did you feel any physical sensation when that was occurring?

STONER: Yes.

MARDEN: What was it?

STONER: Like I was being hit with something I couldn't see.

MARDEN: Go on with your story.

STONER: It's time to prepare for the exit. So, I'm glad to leave that room, and I feel I came out of something that was pressurized. Like I was in something that was bouncing me back and forth... externally.

MARDEN: What happens now that the pressure is gone?

STONER: We walk down the hall, and I don't see anyone. No one... none of the other entities.

MARDEN: Which entity are you with at this point?

STONER: The doctor. He said I didn't have much time left after being in that room that operates the craft. He said since I was exposed to that atmosphere I could fit through the opening to exit the craft if I'd give him that opportunity. Now the taller of the Greys has come. I'm told if I'm willing that I can get through the opening, because it will work without the substance. He stands behind me… puts his hands on my shoulders… and I touch the desert floor.

MARDEN: Your body jumped a little bit. What were you experiencing as you were moving to the desert floor?

STONER: I couldn't breathe, and that's all I remember. It was like the wind had been knocked out of me. I could have been under water holding my breath. And I don't see the entity or the craft. (pause) It's moved away. I see the craft.

MARDEN: Can you describe the craft? What did the craft look like?

STONER: I see the bottom, and the middle rim holds it together. There are two parts, and one rotates clockwise and the other rotates counter-clockwise. The whole center section is the entity that operates the craft. It is the center disk. There are lots of lights. They are white, and there are some around the edges and on the bottom. They are yellow, and there is some red, and they actually rotate and rotate until they blend together until you can't tell the colors. It confuses people on the ground as to whether or not it is an aircraft. There is some green. I see the green but it's mostly white… yellowish white. It kind of looks like stained glass up front when you are up close.

As I began to reflect upon her startling memories of being in an alien environment and the detailed information that she recovered, I wondered if this was in fact an artefactual memory of information that had come her way as an abduction researcher. She reassured me that she had never read or heard this information. Still I felt compelled to speculate whether or not it was a product of her imagination. However, I had used all of my skills as a hypnotist to reduce the possibility that she might manufacture false information. Many of her descriptive details were consistent with my knowledge of the interior of a spacecraft. Her description of the ETs fit the mould. But, although I was aware of information pertaining to the biological nature of the craft's central core, I remained sceptical. I was impressed by Denise's descriptive details and the fact that her body had responded to their room's environment. I had to consider the possibility that this might be real. But if it is real, many more issues are raised. What are the ethical values of beings that would produce a biological entity encased in the central core of a craft? Does it have a soul? Is it bio-mechanical—a living computer? Why did Denise sense profound sadness coming from it?

I had spoken with several experiencers that have memories of the craft as a living entity. One experiencer stated, "Biological material is used deep within the energy system of the craft." Another wrote to me in a private communication, "These craft are living entities, much like a bacteria. They live, breathe, function and create. They are grown from what was initially a hybrid framework. The craft are generic, genetically modified structures.

Not all craft have individual operators, but there are certain parts of their DNA replicated." Still another wrote, "The craft seems to have its own intelligence. It can sense its surroundings." This information had not been publicized, yet Denise described little known information that others had shared (anonymously), with me. Perhaps the ETs were passing information to us with regard to their advanced technology—technology that seems nearly impossible to us.

I wish to thank Kathleen Marden for allowing me permission to quote from her book, *The Alien Abduction Files*.

Living UFOs

Through abduction reports, it appears UFOs can be biomechanical with a sentience. George A. Filer III is the New Jersey state director of MUFON and eastern regional director. He has spoken about holding an alleged UFO fragment that possessed the ability to convey a message to Filer:

I was notified that a friend of a George Ikua Wolkind was in possession of an alleged piece of a UFO that crashed in 1947. When George held the relic in his hand, he felt a warm welcoming message. I met the present owner of the relic who had it examined at the University of Delaware Laboratory. It was determined that the relic was very similar to palladium, but exceptionally light for this type of metal. Additionally, the sample was manufactured in a weightless environment or in space.

Ghosts Moving Erratically

Let us now apply the theory of "thinking you want to be somewhere so you are" to ghostly activity. When you die, your bones are buried in a cemetery or your ashes are placed in an urn. If you are the deceased and want to visit your home in spirit, you need to "think" yourself there. You don't walk in ghostly form from the location of your remains to your previous home—*there is no journey*.

If curiosity exists in your afterlife, you would probably want to see who now lives in your previous home, how well your grandchildren are, how happy your spouse is, and who now has your old job. To do this you must "think" yourself into those locations. Ghosts suddenly appear in a location because they have "thought" themselves there. They disappear when they "think" themselves into the next location.

The Palmer House Ghost Appearing

I now wish to describe some prominent encounters in which I experienced ghosts appearing and disappearing. During one memorable vigil in the Palmer House Hotel in Sauk Centre, Minnesota, I was standing behind a hotel bar in the dark, having turned off all the electrical appliances and lights. I asked if anyone could hear me and, if so, whether they would give me a sign. At that exact moment, all of the lights came on behind the bar. I turned the lights off and started the vigil again. This time the atmosphere changed, and my K2 EMF meter spiked into the red with a reading of over twenty-five milligauss.

Suddenly a full-bodied apparition appeared before my eyes in a diaphanous fog. It was a humanoid shape to my left about six feet away. I turned so we faced one another and waited to see what would happen. The ghost started to walk toward me. For a millisecond I tried to work out what I should do next. When it was about three feet away it just dissipated like cigar smoke dispersing.

Seconds later, the apparition reappeared almost on top of me, forcing me to step backward. It began forming into a humanoid shape again, growing and spreading to my left, but this time it never fully formed and disappeared again. It did not appear again.

I later discovered that the author and hotelier Al Tingley, who was the joint owner of the hotel in the 1970s, had published a book

called *The Corner of Main Street* in which he described the same
entity. He had seen the same smoky-grey humanoid moving toward
him down a corridor on the first floor. From the 1950s and 1960s
onward, guests and staff claimed they had seen the apparition. I had
not known about these previous sightings when I observed the entity,
and I was pleased and reassured that I had described the experience
exactly the same way as Al.

The Ghost of an Old Woman

During a childhood summer vacation in 1979, I made a camp in
the dry ditch of a hedgerow that ran along the side of a cornfield
near my grandparents' vacation home on the Isle of Sheppey in the
Thames Estuary, England.

As I walked along the edge of the field, an old woman suddenly
appeared ten feet away. She was less than five feet tall with dark,
Mediterranean skin like a gypsy or a native of Spain. Deep wrinkles
were etched into her face. From head to foot she wore a black,
featureless cloak and hood. She fixed my stare with her coal black
eyes. I did not move or utter a single word for several seconds. I
stood surrounded by thigh-high wheat for miles and had no idea
how this woman had managed to appear out of nowhere.

Suddenly I felt a surge of fear. The old woman seemed
otherworldly... *paranormal.* I turned and sprinted back to the
sanctuary of my grandmother's embrace. After several minutes I
regained my composure and returned to the location of the sighting.
The woman had completely disappeared, and there was no cover
for miles that would hide an old woman walking slowly through the
field. The apparition had been so shockingly out of place that even
now I find it hard to reconcile what had happened.

The following day I witnessed my younger sister running out
of the camp shaking and looking ashen. She had walked the same
trail at roughly the same time as I had. She, too, had witnessed the
sudden appearance of the strange, dark-skinned woman.

The Speed of Thought

How long would it take to make a journey based on the speed of thought? Would a telepathic thought travel at the speed of light, or faster, or perhaps instantaneously?

US Navy Captain Edgar Mitchell was also a NASA astronaut. He piloted the Apollo 14 lunar module and became the sixth person to step on the Moon. Mitchell conducted private ESP experiments during one of his orbits around the Moon. The *Journal of Parapsychology* published the results in 1971 under the title "An ESP Test from Apollo 14."

Mitchell reportedly used random numbers from one to five to communicate information back to his colleagues on Earth. With only his thought, he assigned a Zener card symbol to each number. NASA did not authorize this experiment, so Mitchell had no time allotted to conduct the experiment. Subsequently, the messages guessed by colleagues back on Earth were undertaken before Mitchell had time to send them. This example is the farthest distance a human has tried to communicate a message telepathically, all the way from the moon's orbit.

If the thought messages Mitchell sent back to Earth had traveled at the speed of a radio signal, they would have covered about 186,000 miles in one second. Radio waves travel at the speed of light as they have the same characteristics as light and would travel in a vacuum from Earth to the moon in 1.26 seconds. The question is, would a telepathic message take the same time as light to reach Earth? Light travels in a vacuum at 186,282 mps, and these nerve impulses are tied to our bodies.

It is possible that a thought may travel instantaneously from one person to another at the moment they think it. After all, there are no physical links or thought bubbles that have to take such a journey—no lighthouse-type beam of information travels from one person's forehead to another person.

You may have experienced the common phenomenon of thinking about an acquaintance moments before his or her call arrives on your phone. In these cases, the caller has the "thought" about making the call, and in the time it takes to press the phone's buttons their intention to call has already telepathically arrived in your mind.

I have experienced calling a friend at the same time they tried to call me. This would come as no surprise to a psychic or those with an ability to communicate through thought. But how quickly would we actually arrive in a location after "thinking" ourselves there? Perhaps instantly.

Our thoughts, feelings, and actions rely on the interaction of chemicals in our brains. These interactions enable brain cells to communicate with one another. New research indicates that it only takes a few milliseconds for brain cells to recollect and reuse these chemicals. This endlessly allows for quick communication.

In the body, neurons communicate with each other through a synapse, a tiny space between the cell coverings called membranes. These synapses are very complex, and we are only just learning how to pick them apart to figure out how they work. When sending a signal, a neuron releases chemicals called neurotransmitters into this space. One of the most important parts of this process is how cells recollect molecules and how they are stored. Neurotransmitters send dozens of signals per second and are used repeatedly.

A report published on May 25, 2013, in the *Proceedings of the National Academy of the Sciences*, outlines the findings of experiments conducted by John Hopkins scientists seeking to measure rates of comprehension. By using a grid of 174 electrodes, monitored volunteers demonstrated they could start to understand a picture within 300 milliseconds. To fully comprehend the picture required an additional 250-450 milliseconds of brain activity depending on the individual. This provides a "thinking" time of 550 to 750 milliseconds. The speed of comprehension of objects already familiar to the volunteers was faster. Communicating through thought, it seems, may be as quick as *I think it, you have it.*

Is it possible, then, that a ghost or alien could take themselves anywhere they wanted to go in the 550 milliseconds it takes to think about being there? If aliens shared the same brain functions and chemistry as humans, going to the local shopping mall, a restaurant in Paris, or the other side of the galaxy would happen almost instantaneously. If ghosts traveled in similar fashion, it suggests that the electricity used for the process of thinking continues to exist after death, since the brain would have long since decayed and rotted. I will cover this theory in more detail in the Energy chapter.

How far away a destination is would be irrelevant under these circumstances. If the shopping mall is ten miles away, it will take 550 milliseconds to travel ten miles. If our closest star outside of our solar system is Alpha Centauri C at 4.24 light years away, it will take 550 milliseconds to visit Alpha Centauri C. The time to think about being in these places is so short, it may seem at times that you are in two places at once—if you skip between thoughts. This theory provides an answer to the paranormal phenomenon of doppelgangers, the apparitional double of a living person. I will cover this concept in more detail in the chapter on Time Travel.

UFOs in Two Places at Once

In her book *Mosaic of Extraterrestrial Experience*, November Hanson discusses the idea that UFOs can be in two places at the same time:

> Another intriguing thought is a craft being a conduit between the two dimensions. It is actually in both places at the same time. The interior is the hyperspace to move from point A to point B.

Of all the theoretical ways for ghosts and UFOs to travel, it would seem that "thinking" their way to other places is the most likely, based on the restraints of distance and the lack of physicality. An important consideration is that UFOs and ghosts travel in exactly the same way.

Teleportation and Remote Viewing

There are many options to consider when dealing with the concept of *thinking you want to be somewhere so you are.* Is the entity physically moving as a result of the thought, or staying at location A and just projecting itself to location B like a mirror of itself? Alternatively, in the case of a UFO, does the craft in which we are traveling remain at location A or duplicate itself at location B with us inside? With a ghost, there is nothing left in location A because the individual is dead, and the body has long since disappeared; by default, then, the ghost must be moving to location B fully and not leaving anything behind in location A, which would contain bones, ashes, or nothing at all.

To describe the strange disappearances and appearances of anomalies, American writer Charles Fort coined the word *teleportation* in his 1931 book *Lo!*. The word derives from the Greek word *tele* meaning *distance* and the Latin *portare,* which means *to carry.* Teleportation is a mechanical process, not esoteric. It is the hypothetical method of transportation in which matter or information is dematerialized at one point and re-created at another. Nothing is left behind.

The trouble with teleportation has always been that in order to send a physical being from location A to location B you have to destroy them in A so they can be re-created. This raises many questions about what happens to non-physical characteristics if they are destroyed in A. If only a physical copy of the teleported being arrives in location B, what happens to our feelings, thoughts, ideas and memories?

This theory is in contrast to the concept of astral projection or remote viewing, in which the traveler stays in the same place physically but explores a destination outside of the body. In astral projection, consciousness is placed into the astral plane. In remote viewing, consciousness is placed into the earth plane, or earth projection. These two planes have different vibrations. Astral vibrations are finer and include a much broader range of frequencies; the bandwidth for perception is greater for colors, sounds and entities. Both planes require the individual to remain physically at a location while undertaking an esoteric journey. Both assume the existence of a soul or consciousness, which is called an astral body and is separate from the physical body and can travel throughout the universe where it interacts with other astral bodies and is capable of implanting ideas and messages.

Both practices—astral projection and remote viewing—seek impressions about distant or unseen targets using extra-sensory perception or the mind. Neither practice allows individuals to interact with another being or thing at point B—or even to be seen—hence the term *viewing*.

Remote Viewing

Physicists and parapsychologists Harold E. Putoff and Russell Targ researched remote viewing (RV) extensively at the Stanford Research Institute. Their work in the mid-1970s attracted attention and funding from the US Central Intelligence Agency, which was looking for a military application for psychic phenomena. Conducted in secret for almost twenty years and with a twenty-million-dollar budget, the work was called the Stargate Project. Some of this work explored the limits of what RV could achieve and how to improve the quality and consistency of results. Other work involved training operatives to collect intelligence information against foreign adversaries.

Governmental funding of the effort ended in 1995 after the collapse of the Soviet Union and with the official belief it had failed to produce any significant or useful intelligence information. Those involved, however, have published books outlining successes achieved during the project, including the accurate prediction of a launch date for a newly constructed submarine in January 1980 and the predicted release of hostages in the Middle East along with accurate descriptions of their medical problems. One project member received a Legion of Merit in 1984 for determining, through the use of RV, 150 essential elements of previously unknown information.

There are some key areas that differentiate RV from the concept of *thinking you want to be somewhere, so you are*. Remote viewers are not visible at the locations they travel to; as we know, ghosts and UFOs are visible and interactive. With RV the viewer is still physically at the location from where he or she started the process, having traveled ethereally to the new location. The process is termed remote viewing because the viewer is remote and removed from the location being observed.

An Esoteric History of Travel

The concept of moving across vast distances without mechanical assistance is not new. It has been with mankind throughout our history and is documented in many religious and cultural texts. It is rooted in worldwide religious accounts of the afterlife in which consciousness or soul leaves the physical body and travels in a dream body or astral body into higher realms.

When Buddha left what is now Patna during his last journey in around 554 BC, he had to cross the Ganges River in order to reach Vesāli. The river at this location is over a half-mile wide. Without a boat or any other way of crossing the river, the Buddha and his monks vanished from the bank and reappeared on the opposite side in front of many eyewitnesses.

Kefitzat Haderech, meaning *contracting the path*, is a Hebrew phrase and a Jewish Kabbalic term. It refers to the concept of traveling quickly between two points separated by a long geographical distance. The Talmud describes three biblical instances where this took place.

Tayy al-Arḍ (*the folding-up of the earth*) is an Arabic phrase for thaumaturgical teleportation in the Islamic religion. The term describes the concept of traversing the earth without moving the ground under one's feet.

Instances of supernatural transportation also appear in the Bible:

Acts 8:39-40

The Spirit of the Lord caught away Philip... But Philip was found at Azotus.

Jesus appeared out of thin air on several occasions. The term *appeared* would indicate he manifested himself from the invisible to the visible—from a spirit realm into the physical realm.

Luke 24:34

...and saying, "It is true! The Lord has risen and has appeared to Simon."

Mark 16:9

When Jesus rose early on the first day of the week, he appeared first to Mary Magdalene, out of whom he had driven seven demons.

Mark 16:12

Afterward Jesus appeared in a different form to two of them while they were walking in the country.

Also, within Catholic teaching, we find the concept of bilocation, the phenomenon of being in two places at once. Several Christian saints and monks were able to master this skill, including St. Anthony of Padua, St. Ambrose of Milan, and Padre Pio of Italy. It was also documented that St. Alphonsus Maria de'Ligouri was seen at the bedside of the dying Pope Clement XIV in 1774, even though Alphonsus was incarcerated in a cell four days' distance away.

A Spanish Soldier in Mexico

Stories of teleportation over vast distances exist outside of ancient religious texts. The *New Cutting Edge Elementary Workbook,* by Pearson Education Limited, documents the legend of a confused Spanish soldier:

> On October 10, 1592, a soldier appeared outside of the royal Palace in Mexico City, Mexico. He was not wearing a recognizable uniform and held a different firearm. Upon questioning he replied he was Spanish and had the task of guarding the governor of Manila's palace, due to the governor general's assassination that very night. Manila is the Philippines and 8,900 miles from Mexico City—a long journey even by today's standards. The soldier had no idea how he arrived clearly in a state of bewilderment. The church authorities declared the Spanish guard possessed by the Devil and placed him in jail—they did not know what else to do with him.

> Two months later a Spanish ship arrived from Manila bringing news of the governor's assassination on the day the Spanish guard appeared—corroborating his story. A Philippine official onboard the vessel also recognized the man. The released soldier went back to Manila using traditional means.

The soldier did not want to be somewhere else and the thought had not occurred to him, but this story embraces the concept it could be possible—even if the individual did not know how it happened.

New Hampshire Child

Many unsubstantiated stories exist that purport to show the phenomenon of teleportation. One example is from 1966 in Dover, New Hampshire. That August, a four-year-old girl named Holly Flynn was very sick. A few weeks earlier she had begun to complain to her parents of feeling tired and having neck pain. Then she developed a serious fever and vomiting. Her concerned parents noticed her pale, yellowing complexion. When she started having seizures, the Flynn family rushed their daughter to a hospital where she was diagnosed with meningitis, a serious but treatable bacterial infection.

She was administered the appropriate antibiotics but remained ill for several days. During her recovery, the family experienced an unexplained phenomenon. One night around ten p.m. the nurse on duty entered Holly's room to check on her progress. She was shocked to see that the girl was not in bed. She checked around the room, in the bathroom and around the hallways, but Holly could not be found. Meanwhile, at the Flynn home, Holly's older brother, Mike, was in his room when he heard what he thought was his sister in the room next door. Confused, he went to Holly's room and found her in the middle of the floor playing with her blocks; she was wearing her hospital dressing gown. He asked what she was doing home. She replied simply that she missed being home and wanted to play with her toys.

Mike rushed down the stairs to get his parents, but when they reached Holly's room she was gone. Her blocks, however, were still in the middle of the floor. At the hospital, the nurse who had sought help in searching for Holly returned to the girl's room and found her asleep in bed as if she had been there all evening. The Flynn family and staff at Wentworth-Douglass Hospital confirmed Holly's brief disappearance in the hospital and her appearance in her bedroom at exactly same time.

UFO Sighting and Car Teleportation

In South Africa, a couple reported a UFO sighting from inside their car just before they lost control of the vehicle, which continued at high speed across the African plain. For five hours, except for a few short intervals, they were unable to steer or brake and felt an unusual coldness within the car. Under hypnosis, one of the individuals stated that a humanoid from the UFO had entered their car and was with them in the back seat during the entire journey.

UFO investigators have files on at least five other cases of alleged automobile teleportation on the continent of South America. In three instances, individuals found themselves suddenly transported thousands of miles from Argentina and Brazil to Mexico. These cases are difficult to investigate as many of the published reports simply lack significant details. Nevertheless, the reports suggest a pattern of events.

Portals and Wormholes

Fictional literature provides many examples of doorways that lead to new dimensions and strange lands. In *The Lion, The Witch and The Wardrobe* by C.S. Lewis, a gateway to a parallel universe is locked away at the back of a wardrobe. In *Alice's Adventures in Wonderland* by Lewis Carroll, when Alice wants to visit the alternative reality of Wonderland, she squeezes herself down a rabbit hole.

Portals are theoretical doorways of energy through which both aliens and spirits may enter or exit a location—doorways that connect two distant locations separated by different dimensions or space-time. They act as an alternative method of traversing space and link the living physical world with the realm of the dead.

Séances Opening Portals

Séances and Ouija boards open portals for spirits to pass back and forth. These practices of spiritualism developed in the middle and upper classes throughout the latter half of the nineteenth century. Spiritualism reached its peak by the early twentieth century at which time it had over eight million adherents throughout the US and Europe. The rapping sounds, playing of musical instruments, automatic writing and divination were presented as tangible evidence of communication with the dead, and practical-minded Americans found the theatrics appealing. The Ouija board, with its distinctive alphabet design, was patented and introduced in 1890. Before this time, letters were drawn on a table or plate.

Sauk Centre Séances

The site of the Sauk Centre House in Sauk Centre, Minnesota, is notoriously haunted and now called the Palmer House Hotel. Through historical research, I discovered that séances were held there in the nineteenth century. With the town's citizenry providing a willing audience, J.L. Potter and H.H. Smith conducted five séances during the week of August 9, 1872, as reported in the Sauk Centre Herald:

> Spiritualism—Messrs. J.L. Potter and H.H. Smith, who lectured here last fall, are coming again and will give four or five lectures, commencing August 9th.

The Sauk Centre House in Sauk Centre, Minnesota, c.1870.

The following year, Mr. Potter returned and again performed in front of an enthusiastic Sauk Centre audience:

> December 6, 1873: Spiritualism—J.L. Potter, trance speaker, who travels under the auspices

of a State Society or organization of Spiritualists lectured here five evenings ending on Sunday last. Our Citizens manifested their usual liberality and willingness to hear new theories and doctrines by a large attendance.

The practice of conducting séances in large numbers could have opened many portals that spirits could now use to access the property.

The LeDuc Estate, Hastings, Minnesota

William LeDuc built the LeDuc house in 1866 and held regular séances in the parlor and dining room. William used a "talking board" during his séances. Through this practice, it is possible he opened a portal for any number of spirits to travel without discrimination. It is therefore possible the reported hauntings of the LeDuc house have no relation to the family or the building.

The Boggs' House Portal

In 2012, I investigated the Boggs' house in Mantorville, Minnesota. Simeon Boggs was born in 1825 into slavery in Missouri and was a veteran of the Civil War. He fought in the colored troops Company G regiment of the 65th USC Infantry under the leadership of General A.J. Edgerton. He had married Flora, who was from a plantation near Clinton, Louisiana, during the course of the war.

Mr. and Mrs. Boggs followed General Edgerton when he returned to Mantorville in 1867. They'd set up a home and became the first African-Americans to reside in town. They lived together for thirty-six years until Flora passed in 1903. Simeon died two years later and was laid to rest beside her in Evergreen Cemetery, Mantorville.

The current owner of the house asked my team to investigate paranormal activity that had been occurring on the property. She had used a digital voice recorder to document the spirit voices she'd heard throughout her home. Upon my arrival, she handed me a CD containing hours of recorded material.

The basement of the Boggs' house was the most paranormally active part of the building. As I began my investigation, I stood in the darkness at the top of the basement stairs looking down into the blackness I believed to be a portal. I felt a constant draught, perhaps the sensation of entities traveling by me in both directions on a kind of supernatural highway. Such a thoroughfare could explain why the town of Mantorville has more than its fair share of hauntings. It was clear that the constant spiritual traffic was a genuine issue for the homeowner.

The portal obscured my view of the floor at the bottom of the stairs, and I experienced dizziness and vertigo. I believed that if I jumped from the top of the stairs into the void I would not have reached the floor below but instead would have disappeared from this dimension. I discussed with my team the danger of leaving an unfiltered gateway to the spirit world without any knowledge of who or what was coming through it. The team's pastor delivered a Christian ceremony to block the portal. I suspect séances were once held in the house and had created this phenomenon.

The Loon Lake Portal

I investigated the pioneer Loon Lake Cemetery in Jackson County, Minnesota during the fall of 2014. While there I had an interesting conversation with a spirit called Mary Jane Terwillegar who had died in 1880. I asked her via the ghost box if she was troubled by my presence.

"Get out!" she shouted.

"Why would you say that?" I asked.

"Portal!" came her surprising reply.

I believe Mary Jane was trying to warn me of a portal that existed in the cemetery and was asking me to leave for my own safety. If there was a portal there, it would certainly explain the reported phenomenon of shadow figures wandering randomly through the grounds. During my interaction with Mary Jane I had seen a shadow figure moving around the perimeter of the cemetery on the inside of the fence. I knew that teenagers had brought Ouija boards into the cemetery over the years and wondered if these actions had created a portal. I asked once more to gain clarification.

"Is there a portal in this cemetery, a doorway that spirits can come through without any filter or discretion?" I asked.

"Yes!"

"Would you like it closed up?"

"Yes!" she replied once more.

Loon Lake Cemetery in Jackson County, Minnesota.

A Fourth Dimension

If evidence suggests that spirits can travel through portals, I believe it is possible that aliens can also access this method. Ufologists believe that portals can answer the question of how aliens access the expanse of the universe. November Hanson documents her beliefs in the book *Mosaic of the Extraterrestrial Experience*:

> We still do not have a clear indication where these beings come from. Are they intelligent life in a fourth-dimensional world? Perhaps they are travelers who can use, work and travel through the hyper-dimensional environment, even if they were from another planet? Are they us from the future? Is it even possible they evolved here on earth and have always been with us? After researching, looking into and reading about a fourth-dimensional reality I feel this seems the most plausible location to start. I have read material from various professionals in physics, watched videos on how to describe a four-dimensional reality and the transitions between the two environments. I have even gone and looked at geometric models that try to give a visual on what the fourth dimension looks like.

Hanson continues to explain how aliens appear to move in a different way to us due to the fourth dimension:

The Greys seem to move fast, be sluggish, and float in some cases. In the fourth dimension you can move in any direction, time relative to our own probably does not exist. This might explain why they can appear to move very rapidly or incredibly slow and when people are gone they seem to misplace a few hours here and there.

Dimensions Bleeding Together

I experienced two dimensions bleeding together during an interaction via the ghost box in a hotel basement in Minnesota. I turned on the ghost box to start a conversation with any spirits that were present.

"Is anyone there who wishes to talk to me?" I asked.

"Who is that?" a woman's voice said.

"My name is Adrian Lee, and I am a historian. I want to chat with you."

"What are you doing in my home?" she asked in a distressed manner.

"I am not in your home. I am in the basement of a hotel."

"Stop, you're scaring me!"

"Why am I scaring you?"

"You are in my lounge. If you don't leave I'll call the police!"

"I didn't mean to scare you."

"Please leave me alone!"

Due to the woman's anxiety and concern I turned the ghost box off and stopped the vigil. The woman genuinely believed I was talking to her from inside her home even though I had conducted the investigation in the basement of a nineteenth century hotel. Clearly, some sort of bleed or crossover had taken place between the hotel location and the location of the woman.

Portal in Oregon County, Missouri

Ted Phillips has conducted paranormal investigations on three farms since 1998 in a small Missouri area he calls Marley Woods. This location has provided multiple landing sites, group UFO sightings, cattle mutilations and force fields. There have been 184 witnesses of these events throughout the history of the site and over 500 events or happenings. Phillips has also documented, with 14 witnesses, what he believes to be a portal. He said to me, "It's like you are looking into a doorway to another dimension."

2232233222232322222222

Phillips has seen strange, hairy creatures at the site and believes the alien beings can come and go at will through the portal. The family living in the farmhouse has seen similar occurrences with objects coming out of the portal. Many of these have been captured on video.

UFOs Using Portals

John Carpenter is a psychiatric therapist and hypnotherapist based in Branson, Missouri. He has a degree in Psychology and a master's degree in Social Work from Washington University in St. Louis, Missouri. He has spent a lifetime studying ufology and documented his findings on how UFOs travel in the essay "Accepting the weirdness coming through dimensional openings: Hunt for the Skinwalker pulls it all together."

When humans learn to crawl out of the dimensional holes that lead to our own ant farm, then we, too, might experience a larger world around us.

Carpenter writes this about the strange creature that came through the portal in Missouri:

> "Openings"—in the sky, air, and ground through which creatures, craft, and humanoid beings seemed to enter and depart in the blink of an eye. On one occasion scientists watched a Bigfoot creature run at top speed across the terrain as if being chased by some invisible predator. As it ran, the creature disappeared; it seemed to slip through an invisible doorway. One evening, an orange glow in the sky became an "opening" through which observers saw blue sky. As they watched, a disc-shaped craft flew out of that "other sky" at high speed into the Utah night sky. This "open rift" in our sky appeared quite often. On yet another occasion two scientists watched with night-vision equipment as a "tunnel

of pale yellow light" expanded to allow a 400-lb
humanoid to pull itself up and into our world!

What gets my attention is that each type of phenomena seemed
to appear and disappear through "invisible doorways" or openings
from one dimension into another. Are diverse and seemingly
unrelated phenomena simply using the same kind of dimensional
openings to enter and exit our world?

Wormholes

The German mathematician Hermann Weyl proposed wormhole theory
in 1921 in connection with the mass analysis of electromagnetic field
energy. But it was not until 1957 that American theoretical physicist
John Archibald Wheeler introduced the term "wormhole." Many
ufologists believe aliens can use wormholes to access the universe.

Wormholes are a hypothetical topological feature of space-
time that offer a shortcut through space. A wormhole is like a tunnel
with two ends, with each end at separate points in the universe.
Wormholes that cross in both directions are "traversable wormholes"
and could be possible if matter, with the density of negative energy,
could stabilize them.

Unlike a portal, there is no observational evidence for a
wormhole. But on a theoretical level wormholes provide a valid
solution to the equations of the theory of general relativity because
of their robust theoretical strength. Thus, wormholes have become
a physics metaphor for the teaching of general relativity. Physicists
have not found any existing processes that could form a wormhole
naturally in the context of general relativity, although the quantum
foam hypothesis is sometimes used to suggest that tiny wormholes
might appear and disappear spontaneously at the Planck scale.
Stable versions of such wormholes have been suggested as dark
matter candidates.

John Wheeler discusses the existence of wormholes in the
book *Annals of Physics*:

> This analysis forces one to consider situations...
> where there is a net flux of lines of force, through
> what topologists would call "a handle" of the
> multiply connected space, and what physicists
> might perhaps be excused for more vividly terming
> a "wormhole."

Particles at the Large Hadron Collider have been seen to pop in and out of existence and may be from other dimensions. In theory the Large Hadron Collider could also produce unparticles, a possible source of dark matter. In theoretical physics, unparticle physics is a speculative theory that conjectures a form of matter cannot be explained in terms of particles using the standard models of particle physics. This created energy may be so focused that even the fabric of space-time may be pulled apart to create a wormhole that would take us instantly to another star. To travel back in time we would simply have to attach one end of the wormhole to a spaceship and fly around at nearly the speed of light for a while—time slows down for a spaceship traveling at this speed—then jump through the wormhole. If the spaceship flew for five years, only six months would have passed within the wormhole, so if you jump through it to the alien star, then fly back to Earth on another spaceship, you would arrive three months before you left. This method requires technology far beyond what we currently have, but there are stars billions of years older than ours and other lifeforms may be able to travel in time.

Black Holes as Wormholes

In the 2016 scientific paper "Physical Review Letters," theoretical physicist Stephen Hawking published "Physical Review Letters," a new theory proposing that the heart of the simplest type of electrically charged, non-rotating black hole is a very small spherical surface. This acts as a wormhole, a doorway or tunnel through the fabric of space-time.

This theory naturally resolves several problems in the interpretation of electrically-charged black holes (MECOs). In the first instance, we resolve the problem of the singularity since there is a door—the wormhole—at the center of the black hole through which space and time can continue. The wormhole predicted by the scientists' equations is smaller than an atomic nucleus but gets bigger as more electrical charge is stored in the black hole. A hypothetical traveler entering the black hole could be stretched thin enough to fit through the wormhole like a strand of cotton threaded through the eye of a needle.

Hawking also argues that black holes aren't the eternal prisons we once thought. He claims you can travel through a black hole and survive, although you would probably come out the other side in a different universe, and there would be no going back.

UFOs Move through Wormholes

Ufologist John Carpenter explains the possibility that UFOs could traverse the universe by accessing wormholes in his article "Accepting the weirdness coming through dimensional openings: Hunt for the Skinwalker pulls it all together":

> Our world is the dimension we can visibly see with our human eyes, but it is not the total of all that could be seen around us. The proximity of other dimensions perhaps suggests that UFOs do not, in fact, travel great distances across the universe to get to earth. Not to sound Star-Trekky, but perhaps the UFOs take a wormhole, make a dimensional leap—and, they're here! Everybody will take a short-cut if they can find one!

Physical or Nonphysical?

If you can be in two places at once, and can "think" yourself into a location, are you physical or nonphysical? First, let's consider whether UFOs and ghosts are actually physical in nature. The evidence suggests that UFOs are solid and have a physicality. There are several types of physical evidence typically presented at landing sites such as burnt ground, weight depressions left in the soil, the flattening of grass or crops, dehydrated earth, and high levels of unexplainable radiation.

UFOs are Physical

Aliens can stand inside a physical UFO, despite the fact they have to "think" it to a specific place in time and space. It would seem possible, then, that UFOs can be physical but also travel instantaneously with thought much like a ghost is able to show elements of physicality in spirit away from the remains of its flesh and bones. It is interesting that aliens do not fall through the floor of a UFO that has arrived by means of thought, and abductees report a physical vehicle that they enter and in which they can move around. This is similar to the way ghosts can travel through walls but don't fall through the floor when they walk. It seems that UFOs and ghosts can be both physical and nonphysical.

Transition of Abductees into Physical Alien Environment

November Hanson documented the physicality an abductee experienced when taken aboard a UFO. She reported in her book *Mosaic of the Extraterrestrial*:

> Then there were those who had a more physical description of the transition. I felt much lighter, nauseated and static. There was a temperature change to a cooler environment or felt extremely cold. It was a place of horrific fear. I felt numb to it all. There is a lack of sound.

The Claude Edwards Case

The exterior of a UFO also exhibits physical qualities. Ted Phillips documented his first landing case in the winter of 1967 at a farm near Tuscumbia, Missouri. It presented a UFO as a solid, physical vehicle that left signs of impact on the surrounding earth.

Just after sunrise, a sixty-four-year-old farmer named Claude Edwards walked across his field to feed his cattle. The cows were all gazing in one direction, so he turned to see what had caught their attention. Edwards was shocked to see a UFO sitting in the adjacent field 160 feet away. Edwards described the massive vehicle as a greyish-green, mushroom-shaped object perched atop a circular tube. It had a metallic surface that was smooth and seamless like shiny silk. He estimated the curved top of the craft to be eighteen feet in diameter and eight feet at the apex. The stem-like tube supporting the craft was constructed of the same material as the dome. There were evenly spaced oblong portholes twelve inches long and spaced at twelve-inch intervals. Edwards believed the portholes did not function as windows. A dazzling array of oscillating colors was emanating from behind them.

Edwards also witnessed a group of tiny alien creatures swarming beneath the object. They were three feet tall with greyish-green skin, similar to the color of the UFO. They had no visible neck and were either wearing goggles or had large, wide-set, black eyes. There were dark protuberances where their noses and mouths would have appeared on human faces; this could have been a breathing apparatus or some kind of protective device. The aliens buzzed around beneath the craft with arms swinging frantically like little green penguins.

Edwards climbed the first gate and started walking directly toward them. He reached a second gate and saw the creatures become agitated. He picked up two large rocks as he approached the craft, intending to puncture the hull and keep the UFO from taking off. Within fifteen feet of the vehicle, Edwards was prevented from getting closer by what felt to him as an invisible wall, a pressure he could not push through.

Unable to strike the vehicle with the rocks, Edwards instead threw one of them at the UFO. It bounced off the hull without making a sound or any noticeable mark. He threw the second rock harder, and it skimmed off the shiny surface like a stone skipping over a lake, indicating the vehicle was solid. The aliens scurried behind the shaft supporting the craft and into the UFO. The craft twice tilted toward Edwards before launching silently into the sky at speed. It leveled off and flew in a northeasterly direction.

Field investigator Ted Phillips interviewed Edwards and photographed the trace evidence left behind, including the soil indentations of the support tube. This evidence indicates a heavy, physical craft.

Claude Edwards wanted to remain anonymous until after his death. He never sought publicity and never gained any financial reward from his encounter.

Radar Evidence

The physicality of UFOs allows radar operators to document their presence. Scientific equipment can record and register their physical presence. The air force, marines, navy, army, and civilian authorities in the United States and abroad have tracked UFOs on radar.

As far back as the late 1940s, Air Force Colonel Charles Brown documented in Project Grudge the recording of UFOs by ground and airborne radar with confirmation through ground and airborne visual contact. Project Grudge was a short-lived project intended to investigate UFOs. Grudge succeeded Project Sign in February 1949 and was eventually replaced by Project Blue Book. The project ended formally in December 1949 but continued in a minimal capacity until 1951.

On October 15, 1948, one of the earliest recorded UFO radar encounters happened in Fukuoka, Japan. Using data provided by an airborne radar operator, a Northrop P-61 Black Widow fighter made six attempts to intercept a UFO. Every time the pilot tried to engage the UFO it accelerated and passed out of range. The radar operator estimated that on three of the sightings the UFO traveled seven miles in approximately twenty seconds at a speed of about 1,200 mph. The UFO occasionally maneuvered up and down out of radar elevation limits.

A combined radar and visual sighting in September 1954 became the first UFO encounter prominently reported in the Australian press. A pilot of a Hawker Sea Fury fighter from Nowra Naval Air Station visually observed two UFOs in his air space as he flew from Canberra to Nowra. The pilot described the UFOs as flying saucers traveling at speeds greater than the Sea Fury. The Nowra ground radar operator witnessed three separate returns on the scope.

The Bentwaters and Lakenheath Radar Incident

A UFO encounter took place in 1956 involving Bentwaters and Lakenheath ground radar installations in England. This incident represents ground and air radar contact combined with both ground and airborne visual observations. The UFO Subcommittee of the

American Institute for Astronautics and Aeronautics (AIAA) published details of the encounter in the *Journal of Astronautics and Aeronautics* in September 1971.

On August 13-14, a US Air Force noncommissioned officer night-watch supervisor at the Lakenheath, England, Radar Air Traffic Control Center (RATCC), received a telephone call from the Bentwaters Ground Controlled Approach (GCA) radar installation. A fast-moving object had been observed on their scopes traveling at four thousand mph. The UFO was the size of a normal aircraft target.

The caller said that the control tower at Bentwaters had also reported seeing a bright light passing over the field from east to west at an altitude of four thousand feet. At the same time, a pilot of a C-47 aircraft had reported a bright light streaking under the aircraft and traveling east to west at terrific speed. The UFO made several changes in direction but always in a straight line with no apparent acceleration or deceleration. A De Havilland Venom interceptor scrambled and locked guns on the UFO with its radar fire-control system. Lakenheath RATCC then informed the pilot that the UFO had made a swift circling movement and was now behind the Venom. The pilot attempted numerous evasive maneuvers but was unable to lose the UFO.

Declassified Radar Reports

The latest batch of UFO files from the British National Archives includes a memorandum on "aerial phenomena" prepared for a meeting of the Cabinet Office's Joint Intelligence Committee in April 1957. The files show that modern reports of UFO sightings reached a peak in 1996. According to an Air Ministry note, four incidents involving UFOs tracked by RAF radar remained "unexplained." In each case, unusual behavior of the radar blips in terms of course, speed and heights were reported. Attempts were made to categorize the cause of these sightings to known aircraft nearby, inexperienced operators, or spurious echoes of unexplained origin. The files also contained dozens of UFO sightings reported to the Ministry of

Defense between 1995 and 2003, including more than six hundred reported sightings in 1996 alone.

Seven UFOs Recorded on Radar

US Air Force Sgt. Chuck Sorrells was present at the Edwards Air Force Base in 1965 when seven UFOs appeared overhead for a period of approximately six hours. The objects moved in a bizarre fashion at great speed, making sharp right-hand turns and other erratic maneuvers that were recorded on numerous radars and observed by several witnesses. A jet was scrambled to intercept the UFOs, but the interception failed.

Alaska UFO Radar Contact

FAA Division Chief John Callahan worked for six years as the head of the Accidents and Investigations Branch of the FAA in Washington, DC. His testimony documented a UFO trailing a Japanese Airlines 747 flight over Alaska for thirty-one minutes in 1986. The same UFO also followed a United Airlines flight until it landed. Visual observations as well as air-based and ground-based radar confirmed the incident. The FAA Administrator, Admiral Engen, hastily organized a briefing the following day. The CIA, FBI, and President Reagan's scientific study team were in attendance. The team members were presented with videotaped radar evidence, audio recordings of air traffic communications and data reports. CIA members informed attendees that the "incident never took place," and all evidence was confiscated. Additional documentation that was not presented at the meeting escaped confiscation allowing Division Chief John Callahan to secure videotape and audio evidence.

The UFO was a giant ball four times bigger than the 747 with flashing lights around the middle. The pilot described the flight of the UFO as bouncing around; this action is consistent with my comments at the beginning of this chapter. Ronald Reagan's Scientific Study team, comprised of three professors, commented that this UFO represented the first time that recorded radar evidence lasted any substantial length of time—over thirty minutes.

The Maxfield House Faucet

Ghosts can present physicality by turning lights on and off, slamming doors, throwing objects, making the sound of footsteps and messing around with faucets as occurred during the Maxfield House investigation.

The 1861 Maxfield House is now a jewelry shop. The owner has experienced many paranormal incidents. One of the most intriguing contacts with a spirit came when she was helping a client choose a ring. During this interaction the owner and her customer were interrupted by the sound of a faucet being turned on in the kitchen at the back of the shop. The owner found the faucet turned fully on though no one else was in the building to do it. She turned the flowing water off and returned to the client. Then, for a second time, the same faucet interrupted them. She turned the faucet off again, and it did not turn on for a third time. I believe the spirit was seeking her attention.

The Volstead House Poltergeist

Three times I investigated the Volstead House in Granite Falls, Minnesota, between October 2017 and March 2018. Andrew Volstead purchased the 1878 two-story, wooden-framed structure in 1894. Volstead was famous for helping implement the National Prohibition Act of 1919. I was investigating an upstairs bedroom with an EM pump running. I had witnessed many shadow figures in this area and was waiting for an entity to enter the room. Suddenly a static meter and an EMF meter registered an anomaly in the open doorway. Instruments were also recording changes in air pressure and humidity. A fishing bobber I had placed on a display cabinet as a trigger object started jumping and bouncing around the floor in a show of physicality.

The Volstead House in Granite Falls, Minnesota.

The Trimont Stairs

In 2013, I lived in an old wooden house in the town of Trimont, Minnesota. My bedroom was on the ground floor, and the stairway to the second floor was on the opposite side of the wall from the headboard. The house was haunted, and I often heard muffled spirit discussions taking place between two people. On several occasions I heard someone ascending the creaky wooden stairs one step at a time as I sat in bed. I was the only one in the house at the time.

Paranormal Syrup

The Baloun pioneer house in Jackson, Minnesota, possessed some kind of physical presence. When I ascended the tight narrow stairway to the upper level it became almost impossible to walk. It was like trying to wade through paranormal syrup. I felt the same sensation when I investigated the Melrose Historical Society Museum in Minnesota. The Museum previously had been a nunnery, and I could barely stagger along the corridor on the top floor due to the nauseating and gut-twisting energy that felt like dense air I needed to push through. Several skeptical locals were present at the time and agreed they could feel the same thing.

The Baloun House in Jackson, Minnesota.

Physical and Ethereal at the Same Time

Despite their physicality, UFOs and ghosts often behave in an ethereal, nonphysical manner. Craig R. Lang, MS, CHT, published an essay in the *Journal of Abduction Encounter Research* under the title "ET Air Traffic Control, the Logistics of UFO Abduction." He categorized UFOs into two categories—para-physical or physical. In the following statement he pointed out that physical UFOs are easier to investigate:

> For as long as I have been involved in UFO research, the nature of UFO abduction has been a topic of vigorous debate. Over the years I have noted that, excluding skeptics and debunkers, there are least two camps of belief on the topic. One argues that UFO abduction is in some way non-physical or para-

physical in nature. The other—which appears to me to have the largest number of adherents—claims that the entities responsible for UFO abduction are physical beings, coming to Earth in physical craft. Our means to explore scientifically a metaphysical or paranormal model of UFO abduction is very limited. However, a physical "nuts-and-bolts" extraterrestrial hypothesis is something we can more objectively evaluate. From UFO sighting reports and accounts related by abductees, we can estimate the magnitude of the alien effort.

In *Extraterrestrial Odyssey*, Craig R. Lang and William McNeff documented the experiences of abductee Roger Kvande who had described throwing rocks and sticks at a UFO with the following result:

> Rocks and sticks thrown at craft passed right through it.

This is contradictory to the case of Claude Edwards in which thrown rocks bounced off the hull suggesting a UFO can be physical and nonphysical at the same time depending on the immediate needs of the aliens.

November Hanson documented the experiences of an abductee who had described a UFO interior as "nonphysical" in her book *Mosaic of the Extraterrestrial Experience*:

> The abduction environment seems translucent even lacking solidity. Their environment feels like my consciousness is in another location.

Rosemary Ellen Guiley, PhD, published an interview with Ray Fowler in the *Journal for Abduction Research* under the title "Talking with Ray Fowler about UFOs, NDEs, OBEs, time warps, and the 'clock phenomena.'" Ray Fowler is one of the leading international authorities on ufology and abductions, including the celebrated Betty Andreasson Luca case. Fowler's research of Betty's involvement with aliens spanned more than twenty years. Fowler has written many books based on his own abduction experiences. His theories on ufology merge with the paranormal world, including issues such as near-death experiences, out-of-body experiences, other dimensions, extrasensory perception and ghosts. In an interview, he discussed theories on the connection between UFOs the paranormal world:

> UFOs and their entities have para-physical abilities. They materialize into our reality as solid objects. But are able to dematerialize to another coexisting reality.

The entities reported by UFO and near-death experiencers are the same beings witnessed under different circumstances. Both appear human. Both can appear as light bodies. Both use telepathy.

UFO not Recorded by Radar

In March 2018, a UFO presented itself as solid yet undetectable by radar. Two pilots flying different planes above Albuquerque, New Mexico, spotted the UFO flying above their passenger aircraft. The first pilot sent a radio message asking if something had passed over him. He asked, "Was anybody above us, to pass us, about thirty seconds ago?" The air traffic controller simply replied, "Negative." The pilot then exclaimed, "Well something did... UFO!"

A few minutes later, the same air traffic controller asked another pilot in the area if he had seen anything nearby. The controller said, "Let me know if you see anything pass over you here in the next fifteen miles." The second pilot seemed unsure of what had been asked and replied, "If anything passes over us?" The ATC explained, "Affirmative, we had an aircraft in front of you at thirty-seven that reported something pass over him, and we didn't have any targets, so just let me know if you see anything pass over you."

A few minutes later, the American Airlines pilot came back on the channel to confirm he also had experienced a strange encounter. The pilot said, "I don't know what it was, but it wasn't an airplane. It passed us, going in the opposite direction. Something just passed over us, like a... don't know what it was, but it was at least two, three thousand feet above us. It passed right over the top of us."

The controller then asked if it was moving, or hovering, or if it could have been a Google balloon. But the pilot replied, "Doubtful... UFO."

Lynn Lunsford of the Federal Aviation Administration told KOB News in the US:

> We don't have any comment beyond what you hear. Other than the brief conversation between two aircraft, the controller was unable to verify that any other aircraft was in the area. We have a close working relationship with a number of other agencies and safely handle military aircraft and civilian aircraft of all types in that area every day, including high-altitude weather balloons.

The Ability of Aliens to Travel through Walls

William J. Konkolesky is the Michigan MUFON State Director. He has experienced numerous visitations by alien beings. In his book *Raised in Two Worlds*, Konkolesky described a physical alien's ability to travel like a ghost. Konkolesky wrote that he believes this takes place on the astral plane.

Out-of-body abduction may explain the bizarre abilities these creatures are often said to possess, such as walking through walls and levitating their intended targets out of bedroom windows.

An Alien Appearing and Disappearing

In 2016 I interviewed a lady from Minneapolis, Minnesota, called Fiona. She spoke of her own firsthand experiences of aliens appearing and disappearing at will like a ghost. Fiona is a middle-aged, university-educated, down-to-earth mother of two. In January, 2004, she was listening to a late night interview taking place on a popular paranormal talk-radio show based in California. The interview guest expressed the idea that if you wanted aliens to visit you, all you needed to do was ask them to come to you in thought. That evening, Fiona did something that would affect the rest of her life. She sat down at her bedroom desk, gazed into the night sky from her apartment in Woodbury and focused on that very thought. She thought, *if any aliens or spaceships are out there, I would like to see you.* She concentrated on this thought three more times during the following weeks.

By April, Fiona had almost forgotten about these thoughts. One evening, just before midnight, as she lay on her bed in sweatpants and a T-shirt trying to sleep, the atmosphere in the room suddenly changed. Fiona described it as becoming "milky," as in dense and thick with more substance than normal air. She also felt what seemed like a buildup of energy—like a pressure— and a buzzing that seemed to focus her thoughts. This whole process lasted thirty seconds.

Fiona was laying on her left side facing the door and closet in a room illuminated only by her computer monitor. Suddenly she felt and heard something behind her. Her mattress depressed, making a squeaking sound to register the weight and physicality of someone or something sitting down on it. Her first thought was, *oh no!* She turned her head slowly to see what might be on her bed. Just inches from her face, she saw the head of what she believed was an alien. It had no scent, and the limited lighting made it difficult to fully see details of its features.

Fiona could make out the texture of its skin, however, and the shape of its large head, which was domed at the top and became pinched into a pointed chin at the bottom. She later believed she had experienced contact with a type of alien ufologists describe as a *grey.* His nearest eye was large and shaped like a tear drop with the pointed part at the bottom. The rest of the eye reached around its head to give the creature a peripheral vision. Fiona said its eye glowed in differing shades of blue and green giving the impression that it may be communicating something. It had nothing like recognizable human features, and Fiona described it as similar to the head of a fly.

The alien, laying behind her, embraced her with its right arm, which was like a thick stick with long, skinny fingers containing many nodules. She remembered seeing four fingers but was unsure if it had a thumb. She felt the weight of its arm as it laid across her reclining body. Fiona's paralyzing fear prevented her from screaming or fleeing. By the time she looked sharply back to the bedroom door it had gone, suddenly—just as it had appeared. Fiona felt the sensation of the mattress going back to its state without the weight of the alien. She jumped up and turned the lights on to gather her composure.

Though the incident had occurred twelve years earlier, it still clearly felt emotionally raw for Fiona, who had never discussed the incident with her friends and family. Throughout the interview with me, she talked quietly as if fearing that others might overhear our conversation.

Fiona told me that physical trace evidence presented itself during the following week when a neighbor found an eight-foot-diameter circle scorched into the grass directly outside her bedroom window. The line of the circle was four inches in width, suggesting that a vehicle had brought the alien to the vicinity of Fiona's apartment prior to it gaining entry to her bedroom by paranormal means.

Fiona believed she had summoned the encounter due to asking for it through the power of thought. The alien had appeared and disappeared in the same way ghosts manifest and behave, entering her room through the mass of the wall as if it were a nonphysical being, yet registering physicality through the weight on the mattress and the arm placed around her.

Fiona's detailed and educated account was remarkable due to the way she described how the atmosphere changed in her room moments before the manifestation. The buildup of energy and the experience of feeling a dense atmosphere, along with a buzzing sensation and increased pressure, reflect my own experiences of how a location feels before paranormal contact with a ghost.

Fiona believes she has had more visitations after this contact. She would often wake up, she told me, with her clothing on back-to-front, inside out, or in the wrong order.

Aliens Move Abductees Like Ghosts

Paranormal radio host and ufologist November Hanson is also the co-founder of the International Community for Alien Research ICAR. In her ebook *Mosaic of the Extraterrestrial Experience*, she presents the results of an online questionnaire completed by fifty abductees for the purpose of providing a deeper insight into abduction phenomena. In the ebook, Hanson stated that 74 percent of questionnaire respondents described *being drawn* through solid objects. Hanson thinks the abductors are utilizing a technology that rearranges the molecules of solid objects to allow a physical object to pass through another.

November Hanson believes the removal of abductees may not be solely physical but that in some cases only the consciousness is taken through out-of-body travel:

> A staggering seventy-four percent of the people who completed the Grey questionnaire experience reported being drawn through a solid object. They reported being drawn through a window, a wall, or a roof of a house. Equally as impressive is although often times similar not one person described the feeling associated with this experience the same.

Oddly enough, when asked how the Greys appeared to move through the solid object everyone responded in one of four ways such as, effortless, like a ghost, like a hologram or levitated.

Perhaps first we need to be drawn into the fourth dimension. The Grey's can walk right through a wall, a door (without opening it) or, my favorite, through a plate glass window without receiving a single scratch. I thought in the past the most logical explanation would be a technology we do not have that halts atomic movement allowing one to seemingly step through a solid object. If they are coming out of the fourth dimension, all they have to do is walk right in. It is not a problem... apparently it is not a problem for them to take you back with them either. Basically, Mr. Grey is just taking you next door.

Aliens Moving from a Physical Body into a Light

One abductee witnessed an alien transforming from a physical body into a light. Jayna Conkle describes her experiences in the essay "These vermillion-skinned, high-ranking alien females in shiny robes can turn invisible!"

The bodies of the three naked female vermillion aliens were quickly transforming into pure light forms of a pale yellowish color, keeping their body shape. I couldn't see any devices or cause for this light other than the aliens themselves. Neither do I remember hearing any sound accompanying the light. I heard a woman in front of me exclaim, "They've turned invisible!" followed by sounds of surprised agreement from others around her.

Conkle was also able to put her arm through an alien as it passed—reinforcing its nonphysical nature:

> I waited for the walking robe/grey to get close
> enough, then I swept my arm out toward where
> her ankles would be, above the sandals but below
> the robe—and my arm went right through her legs!
> (Though I felt the robe brush my arm.)

Can We Use the Same Method of Transport?

If aliens and ghosts can travel by just thinking they want to be somewhere, how close are we to operating our own vehicles to make this happen? Although we are not able to transport ourselves into a time or a place just by utilizing thought, technology already exists that suggests a process may be available to future generations.

In current experiments, pilots are attempting to control mechanical vehicles solely with the power of thought. The technology used in lie detector tests has proven to control seizures in epileptics and is allowing individuals to control characters on a computer screen via thoughts. A clinical study in 2016 reported that electrodes attached to the index and middle fingers can measure tiny changes in stress via the skin's sweating response. The more stress a person feels, the greater the electrical conductivity of the skin; a sudden increase in conductivity indicates a lie.

Dr. Yoko Nagai of the Brighton and Sussex Medical School modified a lie detector machine so the user's electrical activity could move a character on a computer screen. Patients were able to focus on a character and "will it" to move. The more these patients focused on the task, the faster the characters moved. Once trained, the patients could increase their level of alertness, which helped them to calm their brains and reduce the frequency of seizures.

An initial clinical trial of a technique called Autonomic Cognitive Rehabilitation Training (ACRT) involved twenty-one patients who were required to focus on a computerized fish in an attempt to morph it into a woman. Solely through the use of their minds, the patients not only accomplished this task but were then able to navigate the woman along a beach, up a hill, and through some ruins.

Controlling Planes with Thought

In 2013 the *Journal of Neural Engineering* published a paper that documented the work of the University of Minnesota College of Science and Engineering under the leadership of Professor Bin He. A team of neuroscience researchers demonstrated the ability to fly and maneuver a remote-controlled helicopter using only their thoughts. This process worked by using a sophisticated brain-computer interface that detected thoughts and interpreted them as control signals to direct a helicopter accordingly.

When the controller imagined a helicopter movement, specific neurons in the motor cortex of the controller's brain produced electric currents measurable by the pilot who wore a cap fitted with sixty-four electrodes. A computer translated the signal pattern into a command and beamed it to a robot via Wi-Fi. The process was non-invasive and required no implants or chips to detect the brain signals that were translated into commands.

The computer scientists at Zhejiang University in China are also currently developing a way to fly a drone with just the power of thought.

Military Developments

In 2013, under the headline "The Future of Flight," Tech. Sgt. Mark Kinkade stated that pilots were currently maneuvering craft via helmet-mounted, heads-up displays that projected a virtual reality soundscape of the battlefield arena. Most advanced avionics research in powered flight today falls into three areas, he states—integrating the pilot and the aircraft more comprehensively; aircraft design and function; and aircraft construction. A spokesperson for the Air Force Research Laboratory's human effectiveness systems interface division at Wright-Patterson Air Force Base went on to state, "We're talking science fact. What can we do to improve aircraft today, not fifty years from now?"

Kinkade said the cockpit is an information center, and the pilot has to assess a massive input of data in seconds to determine a course of action. Consequently, developments are underway to make that process easier. This includes brain control of the aircraft—the ultimate in pilot/aircraft cohesion—and look-and-shoot targeting systems.

Two Heads are Better than One

A collaborative study by NASA and the University of Essex showed improvements are achievable when a pilot flying a virtual spaceship is connected through a brain/computer interface with a co-pilot in an exotic mind-meld.

It appears that two heads, or at least two sets of brain waves, really are better than one for this task. Two sets of brain waves are read by an EEG machine and merged together to form a single wave. This wave can then command movements to a spaceship simulator program. The pilots control their ship by concentrating their thoughts on one of eight compass directions to steer in that direction. In experiments using pilots in a computer simulator situation, the team found that the combined brainwaves of a pair of pilots consistently outperformed those flying solo. As a pair of concentrated thoughts are averaged together, some of the distracting background thoughts are cancelled out. Otherwise heartbeats and other involuntary muscle movements can create distortion in a single EEG reading.

Researchers also found that using two sets of brain waves helped to compensate for lapses in attention when one pilot's thoughts drifted to something else, as the human brain is prone to do. This embryonic science could explain why many abductees, as previously discussed, believe aliens pilot UFOs through mass collective thought negating the use of levers, buttons, or steering devices.

Time Travel

The possibility of traveling to a physical destination or one in time by thinking of it explains why ghosts often haunt a past period with familiar surroundings. If I die at age eighty and want to come back in spirit to a time when I was twenty-one, then will my physical self at twenty-one see the ghost of me? Therefore, in other words, is it possible to haunt one's self? There have been many examples of individuals who have seen themselves at differing ages.

A doppelgänger is a paranormal phenomenon in which an individual sees themselves. In his autobiography *Dichtung und Wahrheit,* German playwright Johann Wolfgang Goethe described the experience of seeing an older version of himself pass by on horseback. English writer Izaak Walton claimed that metaphysical poet John Donne, in 1612, saw his wife's doppelgänger in Paris on the night their daughter was stillborn.

Abductees and those experiencing spirit contact have both described similar time manipulations and distortions. Ufologist Yvonne Smith, a graduate in 1990 with a certification from the Hypnosis Motivation Institute, specializes in treating sufferers of post-traumatic stress disorder, especially in the aftermath of alien encounters. In 1992 she founded the Close Encounters Resource Organization (CERO), a monthly support group for experiencers. In her article "They're saying it's my child—I can't believe this is happening!" Smith describes the experiences of a client she called John who lost time after contact with a UFO:

One event bothering John was a Dec. 31, 1980 experience he had while driving California's Highway 5. John was heading to Sacramento to ring in the New Year with his girlfriend. Before the hypnosis began, what John recalled was that shortly after 10 p.m. that night he had spotted a large, dark object coming toward him and moving slowly left to right. When John uneventfully passed the object, he looked behind him, but it was no longer in sight. "I have to see what this is," he commented to himself, and his thought was to pull over. He next remembered his truck engine sputtering and that he felt groggy, as though he had just awakened from sleep, but he was driving, and both hands were on the steering wheel. It struck him as odd that all the holiday traffic was gone, and no other cars were in sight on the roadway. Thinking only a few minutes had passed, he called his girlfriend to tell her about his unusual observation, and was he startled when she was angry with him. He had no idea it was 1 am— three hours later! John's first appointment with me for hypnotic regression was in the winter of 1992; it was to be an exploration which would last many years. In connection with just the 1992 experience on the highway, John and I did six hypnotic regressions, each filled with heart wrenching emotion and sense of loss of control. John was tormented by the thought: "When will this happen again?" John's was a "missing time" event—a term coined by my colleague and mentor, Budd Hopkins, many years ago.

(The first documented "missing time" case was the historic Sept. 1961 double abduction of Betty and Barney Hill.)

During an interview with Rosemary Ellen Guiley, seasoned ufologist and author Ray Fowler described the phenomena of time anomalies experienced by abductees in the essay "Talking with Ray Fowler about UFOs, NDEs, OBEs, time warps and the 'clock phenomena'":

> Witnesses report experiencing time standing still, suspended animation, time effects upon clocks, and lengthy experiences in a short linear time span. Reports also indicate the entities are space travelers uninhibited by the laws of nature experienced in our reality. Their origin is the otherworldly dimension humans report during near death experiences and UFO abductions in an OBE state.

Missing Time from Another Dimension

November Hanson documented the experience of abductees missing time in her book *Mosaic of the Extraterrestrial Experience*:

> The concept of missing time is often associated with abduction. People have also reported other variations in time such as time speeding up, standing still, feeling out of time, and suddenly sensing being someplace else and time slowing down. Why would the time concept be a part of anything? If I understand the whole space time thing correctly, time in the 4th dimension is happening on a variety of axes, and we have been briefly removed from our own linear time and exposed to a different time environment. In my way of thinking this would explain the variations of time experienced.

Lost Time in a Haunted Basement

I personally experienced a distortion of time during a paranormal investigation of the Corner Drug Store building located on the crossroads of Sinclair Lewis Avenue and Main Street in Sauk Centre,

Minnesota. The building at this location was first documented in 1868. During a two-year period, I conducted over 150 investigations at this location, utilizing the services of more than twenty-five skilled paranormal investigators.

We sometimes experienced lost time during any prolonged visit to the west part of the basement. On one occasion I undertook a vigil there and believed, through my own internal clock, that fifteen minutes had passed. To my surprise, and that of my team, I discovered a full hour had elapsed, indicating that I had lost forty-five minutes. This happened more than once.

The Hanson and Emerson Corner Drug Store c. 1896 in Sauk Centre, Minnesota.

It is possible I experienced another dimension that influenced my own timeframe. Time in other dimensions may not move at the same rate as it does in our own dimension. The clock that governs a ghost's behavior may be moving faster than ours, as if the spirit had pressed the fast forward button on a video recording.

We use special (IR) cameras with strobe lights with which to catch fast-moving entities during paranormal investigations. Strobe lights can make fast-moving machinery look static and allow police departments to photograph license plates on moving vehicles.

Ufologist Craig Lang describes the speeding and slowing down of time in his book *Extraterrestrial Odyssey*:

> Einstein's theories deal with some aspects of time travel. As a matter of fact, we are all "traveling" in time, but it is one-way, into the future. We can slow the passage of time for us relative to the rest of the universe by accelerating and traveling at high velocities (speeds).

Conceptually, traveling forward in time is relatively easy; you only need to accelerate to a speed near the speed of light. According to Einstein's theory of special relativity, time will slow down as you reach that point, but only for *you*. Thus, individual entities like ghosts and spirits would be isolated from other entities if they could harness this ability.

Einstein's Special Theory of Relativity

Einstein's theory of special relativity says that time slows down or speeds up depending on how fast you move relative to something else. Approaching the speed of light, a person inside a spaceship would age much slower than his twin at home. This phenomenon has important implications, as any travel faster than light is observable as traveling backward in time.

According to experts on the theory of time travel, it is possible to travel back and forth in time. However, it is difficult and has limitations. It is easier to travel forward in time than backward, and a person traveling backward in time could not go beyond the point in time that the time machine was constructed. In other words, the inventor of the first time machine would not be able to journey backward any significant amount of time.

Of course, a traveler from the future has yet to come back to tour present time to proclaim the achievement—unless the governments of the world are keeping that a secret. Professor Stephen Hawking once organized a special party for time travelers and published the location's latitude and longitude so that visitors from the future could attend. Unfortunately, the professor spent the party by himself.

It is possible that our future time traveling selves would want to be present as spectators for key historic events. Perhaps UFOs could be ourselves from the future observing present events as a history lesson. Science writer Carl Sagan suggested that if time travellers were among us already they might disguise themselves to avoid disrupting the past.

According to scientific theory, a major requirement for time travel is a vehicle capable of obtaining speeds close to and beyond light speed and vast amounts of energy. Extra-terrestrials could possess such vehicles. Ghosts are also able to travel to any destination and time without the need for a physical journey; geographic distance is no restraint. I have felt and seen my deceased grandmother in places she never visited during her physical lifetime. If ghosts are sources of light without a physical body, they should be able to travel at light speed—or as fast as they can think themselves to any location or era.

The concept of time travel and the notion that a ghost can haunt its living self raises many difficult questions. We know that ghosts and spirits can be physical. What happens, then, if a ghost would go back to visit its younger physical self and pushes that younger self down the stairs to her death? When using a time machine, what would happen if you arrived three months before you left and then committed suicide? These are philosophical paradoxes that require deep thought and a second book.

Roman Legionnaires

A famous residual haunting that demonstrates an encounter with spirits from another time period occurred in 1953. The haunting has subsequently been witnessed many times by various witnesses.

This particular encounter was by Harry Martindale, an apprentice plumber, who had gone into the cellar of the Treasurer's House in York, England to install a new heating system. In Medieval times, this historic building now owned by the National Trust was the home of the treasurers of York Minster and served in this capacity until 1547. It then passed through a number of private owners.

Upon reaching the cellar and climbing a ladder, Martindale was startled by the distinctive sound of a distant horn. He wondered how this sound could reach him so far underground, but he carried on with his work. The horn continued to blow, however, each time sounding closer. Suddenly a huge horse emerged through the brick wall of the cellar. Startled, Martindale fell off his ladder and saw that a disheveled Roman soldier rode the horse.

The apparition of the horse and rider was followed by several Roman Legionnaires in rough, green tunics and plumed helmets carrying short swords and spears. The soldiers looked dejected as they marched through the basement. The ghostly men were only visible from the knees up. Martindale soon realized they were walking on an old Roman road buried fifteen inches below the current floor.

The Romans had founded the city of York in AD 71, 1,882 years before Martindale observed the horse and Legionnaires in 1953. If Martindale's shock upon seeing the Roman army in the cellar implanted itself into the metaphysical fabric of the location, then 1,882 years later, in the year 3835, a future worker might see Martindale's ghost falling off a ladder. That would be some serious time traveling!

Ghosts in the Future

An interaction I experienced through the ghost box indicated that an entity was from the future. This occurred in a basement room of the Palmer House Hotel, Sauk Centre, Minnesota, in 2010. I had begun a dialogue by asking for the spirit's name, which was "Michael." I asked if he preferred Mike or Michael. He said, "Michael."

I asked what year he was born. Receiving no reply, I asked in which decade he was born. Again there was no reply. I instructed Michael to say *yes* when I got to the decade in which he was born. I listed decades in chronological order from 1900 until I reached the 2000s. There was no response to any of them. I kept going, more out of curiosity than anything else. When I got to the 2030s he surprisingly said, "Yes."

Confused, I decided to clarify the decade I had just mentioned. "So you were born in the 2030s?" I asked. Once again he replied, "Yes."

"So you are from the future?" I asked.

"Yes," he confirmed.

I believe it is possible a ghost could come from the future. This would be like dying tomorrow and manifesting as a spirit in the 1970s. Many ghosts want to go back to a time and a place at which they were happiest. If ghosts can go forward in time, then perhaps they can go backward by using the same process. Michael claimed to be from the future and had been born in the 2030s, yet I had spoken to him in 2010.

Imagine that a person who was a teenager in 2019 died in 2070. If the spirit of that person wanted to haunt or make contact with the places and people they knew in 2019, they would go back to that date and place.

Now imagine that same person alive in 2019 suddenly making contact with his own ghost, which had returned to that period. That teenager would be talking to a spirit of a person—himself—who died in 2070 but was still very much alive in 2019.

Interviewing Ghosts from Every Era

If ghosts of future deceased can manifest themselves to investigators or scared witnesses in the present, it would suggest a form of time travel. I have contacted and interviewed ghosts and spirits from many historical timeframes and geographical locations. I have written books about these encounters, such as: *Mysterious Minnesota: Digging up the Ghostly Past in Thirteen Haunted Sites* and *Mysterious Midwest: Unwrapping Urban Legends and Ghostly Tales from the Dead.* These books contain over three hundred pages of history obtained through interviews with the dead. The information was provided by the spirits and drove my historical research which uncovered verifiable facts and knowledge that had previously been lost.

The Sweet's Hotel

In 2011, I conducted an investigation in the 1898 Sweet's Hotel in the small town of Le Roy located on the border between Minnesota and Iowa. On the top floor, in a room overlooking Main Street, via the ghost box, I began a dialogue with a male spirit who believed he was in the 1920s. I asked if the room looked the way it had when he was alive, and he replied, "Yes." I asked what he could see in the room, and he described different wallpaper. The bed and other furniture was positioned differently in his description. He also told me the room was full of flowers. I had the impression he was seeing his own wake but was overlooking his physical body, which must have been laid out on the bed.

This incident raises many questions. He saw the room as it was from his own time in the 1920s. He seemed utterly convinced he was in that era. I was investigating the room in the year 2011, so this spirit had either come forward to my time period to interact with me, or I had gone back to his time. The ghost could hear my questions in his time, the 1920s, and I could hear his reply in 2011.

If this spirit was seeing his own wake, he was viewing the world around him after his physical body had died. This means he must have continued a linear chronological progression past the moment he had died, suggesting that spirits can visit the future after their physical passing.

A Spirit Directing Me to Her Grave

In 2016, I investigated the famous haunting of Mary Jane Terwillegar at Loon Lake pioneer cemetery in Jackson County, Minnesota. The local historical society had removed her gravestone due to vandalism, so I did not know the exact location of her burial. I decided to turn on the ghost box and ask Mary Jane to give me directions to her grave.

As I stood on the edge of the undergrowth, I asked, "What way do I need to go to reach your grave?"

"Just go in," she said.

I set off toward the middle of the cemetery and asked her to give me further directions. I have amended the following dialogue slightly so that her body may rest in peace.

"Am I going in the right direction?" I asked.

"Yes."

I continued making my way through the undergrowth.

At last she called out, "Cease!"

I stopped.

"Go back," she added.

I stepped back several paces. "Here?" I asked.

"Yes."

"Which direction should I head now?"

"Right."

I started walking off to my right. "Am I going in the right direction now?"

"Sure, straight," she said.

I kept walking straight ahead.

"That's okay," she continued.

"Am I still going the right way?"

"Yeah."

"Is this close?"

"Nope," she said.

"Clarify that for me."

"I'm here," she suddenly responded.

I stopped walking. "Is this where you are?"

"Yes," she confirmed.

This is a remarkable dialogue when you consider that Mary Jane's spirit was actually giving me directions to her final resting place. She obviously knew the precise location of her burial. This suggests that spirits have a knowledge of what happens after their passing. I suspect we would all want to see who turns up for our funeral and what people say about us.

Bechyn Cemetery

In 2017, I visited Bechyn, a small town in Renville County, Minnesota. I investigated the cemetery of St. Mary's Church and asked if any of the spirits present could direct me to their gravesites.

"Am I facing in the right direction? Yes or no?" I asked.

"Yeah!" came the vague reply in a male voice.

"I am going to walk forward. Can you tell me when to stop?"

"Adrian," the same voice responded.

"Straight on, left or right?"

"Right."

I asked as an affirmation, "Can you give me that again? Left, right or straight on?"

"Right."

"I'm going to keep going right until you say stop."

"Stop!"

"Left, right or straight on?"

"Okay," he responded.

I assumed the spirit wanted me to stop right there. I asked a member of my team to shine a flashlight on the gravestone I was standing in front of.

"What's your first name?" I asked.

"Erwin," the spirit replied.

The flashlight illuminated the name "Erwin" on the gravestone.

Erwin gravestone at St. Mary's Church in Bechyn, Minnesota.

The Schmidt Brewery

An interaction with a spirit at the Schmidt Brewery in St. Paul, Minnesota, was one of my most interesting and curious encounters. In 2008, I investigated the abandoned factory building, and in the derelict basement I witnessed a ghost standing in the gloom. The male apparition was unwilling to communicate, except to psychically explain he was a fireman and his name was Matt.

Several years after this investigation, I uncovered previously lost historical information from which I learned that a brewery worker named Matthew Kohler had died in terrible circumstances in that section of the basement. I naturally believed he was a fireman in the sense of being a firefighter. Indeed, Matthew Kohler was a fireman, but in a different sense, having been responsible for keeping the furnaces fired and the oil lamps lit. The following article appeared in the *Saint Paul Daily Globe* on April 16, 1904:

Matthew Kohler, a Fireman, is Fatally Injured—
Matthew Kohler of 399 Duke Street, while filling a
lamp at Schmidt's brewery, on Seventh Street, about
5:30 last evening, was terribly burned and his injuries
will prove fatal. Kohler was employed in the engine
room as a fireman, and had worked for the brewery for
a number of years, and was considered an efficient and
industrious worker. Just before dark every evening
it was Kohler's duty to draw the fires and see that
everything was in shape for the night. Last evening
he started to fill an oil lamp, and in doing so spilled
some of the oil onto his clothing. In some manner the
oil became ignited and in a second he was enveloped
in flames. Other employees of the concern who were
in the fire room at the time rushed to his assistance
and extinguished the flames, but not before Kohler
had inhaled them. The city hospital was called and an
ambulance was sent to the brewery. At the hospital it
was found that the man had been burned from the lower
part of the body to the top of the head. The physicians
say that his injuries are fatal. Kohler is thirty-seven
years of age, and has a wife and six children.

As predicted, this poor man died in the worst possible
circumstances:

Fireman Dies From His Burns—Matthew Kohler,
the fireman who was terribly burned at Schmidt's
brewery Friday evening, died at the city hospital
yesterday morning at 9 o'clock. Kohler suffered
from inhaling the flames.

Those few sad sentences were a complete vindication of the
psychic process of historically corroborating information resulting
from a paranormal investigation. This experience became the

catalyst for my belief that lost historical information is retrievable from the dead.

Then, in 2018, something remarkable happened during an investigation at Edinburgh Manor in Jones County, Iowa. Edinburgh Manor is a large, abandoned farm building with a history of incarcerating mentally ill patients. It is a sprawling and dilapidated site with few redeeming features. During the last vigil in the boiler room I turned on the ghost box.

"Can you tell me your name?" I asked.

"Matthew," a spirit replied.

"Do you prefer Matthew or Matt?"

"Matthew."

There was something familiar about this spirit. I did not know whether this was a psychic feeling or whether I had recognized his voice.

"Have we met before Matthew?" I inquired.

"Yes."

"Can you tell me where?"

"Brewery," he replied.

"You are Matthew Kohler who died in 1904?"

"Yes."

"Hello, great to meet you again," I said.

I remembered an interaction with Matthew that had occurred ten years before. Finding his obituary based on my previous interview with him had made a big impression on me.

Matthew proceeded to thank me for including him in my book and rediscovering his personal history. He had died in tragic circumstances in 1904 but was able to interact with me in the brewery 104 years after his passing. During that previous interaction, he had gained a knowledge of me in spirit, so when we spoke again at the Edinburgh Manor he remembered me. He also knew about the book I had published in 2012 containing his information. This suggests that spirits can gain wisdom and knowledge after the physical body has gone; they could know who the current president is, for example. Michael had come to talk with me ten years after our first encounter in a building he had never visited during his lifetime. He had traveled to another state 280 miles away. This highlights again the irrelevance of physical distance in spirit.

I believe a spirit needs to have a knowledge of where they want to go in order to think themselves there. Matthew would have had no concept of the Edinburgh Manor and its interior, but had managed to travel there and talk to me in that environment. After she died, my grandmother visited me in Minnesota, which she had never physically visited in her lifetime. She did, though, have a knowledge and memory of *me*, and in spirit visits *me*—wherever I happen to be. In the same way, Matthew accessed *me*. At the time, I just happened to be in the Edinburgh Manor.

I also believe spirits can travel to the location of inanimate objects as well. If a spirit remembers a favorite chair or other possession, he or she can go to the current location where the object is found. This is why antique shops often have so much paranormal activity in them and why modern houses can be haunted; there may be someone else's vase or rug in that home. This suggests that a memory or experience of an object can be implanted into or attached to that object providing residual information for other spirits to recognize.

The Schmidt Brewery in St. Paul, Minnesota, and Edinburgh
Manor in Jones County, Iowa—280 miles apart.

The Battle of Naseby

On June 14, 2008, I investigated the site of the Battle of Naseby
in Northamptonshire. It was on the anniversary of the 1645 Battle
of Naseby, which became a decisive battle of the first English
Civil War. The main army of King Charles I was destroyed by
the Parliamentarian New Model Army, under the command of Sir
Thomas Fairfax and Oliver Cromwell. After a day of fighting, the
Royalist forces incurred six thousand casualties, including one
thousand deaths.

Archaeological evidence, including the recovery of musket balls, suggests the heaviest fighting took place in the vicinity of Long Hold Spinney, about a half-mile behind the Royalist position at the start of the battle. Bodies stayed on the field of conflict for many years after the battle due to the sheer numbers involved and the sparsely inhabited location. Tourists from London often travel there to view the grizzly and gruesome remains.

During the investigation I recorded gunshots on my DVR. Guns are not common in England due to strict firearms laws, so I believe the gunshots to be a residual audio haunting of the battlefield. This phenomenon indicates that time has been manipulated in some way, allowing me to hear sounds of this battle from 1645.

Elizabethan Stable Boy

I encountered an odd apparition as I was beginning a vigil in the barn behind a sixteenth-century Elizabethan building on Main Street of Braintree in Essex, England. This building was once a stable and carriage house. I interacted with the spirit of a boy via the ghost box and EVP recordings. The stable boy was concerned about me distracting him from his work. I could not determine the era during which he lived, but the boy's words suggested a period before motorized transport. The spirit boy was a hostler and described his duties grooming the horses and maintaining the tack. He insisted he would get into trouble if I kept him from his work by asking questions. He seemed genuinely worried that his employer would accuse him of shirking his responsibilities.

RAF Bovingdon

In 2009, I investigated the abandoned Second World War airbase of RAF Bovingdon, Hertforshire, England. Built in 1941 as a standard RAF bomber airfield, it has a main runway of 1,634 yards and two shorter secondary runways. In 1942, the first USAAF tenant at Bovingdon was the 92nd Bombardment Group, which was assigned the role of a B-17 Flying Fortress Combat Crew Replacement Unit. The Ministry of Defense closed the airfield in 1972.

As I stood on the abandoned mile of asphalt, I conversed with a Second World War American bomber pilot through the hissing and popping of the ghost box.

"I'm in trouble," a voice said in an American accent.

"What has happened?" I asked.

"I've lost the engines… tell my wife I love her."

"Where are you from?"

"Austin, Texas."

"Do you have a crew?"

"Yes… ten."

There were ten crew required to fully operate a B-17 bomber. The spirit then proceeded to list the entire crew by name.

Time Travel at the Maxfield House

In 2015, I investigated the Maxfield House in Mankato, Minnesota. During the vigil, I made contact with a spirit in the carriage house via the ghost box.

As I turned on the device, a male voice shouted, "Watch out!"

"Watch out for what?" I asked.

"Ghost!"

"Do ghosts exist?"

"Yes."

"So why do I need to watch out?" I asked.

"You need to understand."

"Understand what?"

"Death!" came the chilling reply. "You need to get this. The afterlife!"

"So what do I need to know about the afterlife?"

"It's real you know…"

I agreed with him and explained that I had spoken with many spirits and ghosts.

"Can you see *us*?" I asked.

"Yes, yes!"

"Who am I talking to?"

"Frank, Frank."

"Hi, Frank. Do you hang out with your friends here in Mankato?"

"Community," he said.

"So you all live in a community?"

"Yes."

"Can you see the jewelry store?"

"No."

"So does the building look like it did when you were alive?" I asked.

"Yes," he said.

Despite talking with me in 2015 and saying he could clearly see me, the current location appeared to him as it had in the 1920s. Clearly, one of us has time travelled. If I am able to engage Frank in a conversation and he can see me, yet I am in the present and he is in the past, something remarkable has taken place. Have I gone back in time, has he come forward, or are we meeting in some kind of middle ground in which our individual timeframes have intermingled?

From the examples above it seems clear that we are capable of time travel today. The only drawback is that we need to be dead. If I died suddenly tomorrow, the implication is that as a spirit I could access people a hundred years into the future. The ghosts of today actually died a century ago. If I died today and came back tomorrow to say hello to my family as a spirit, then I have also time traveled. The lesson is that when the body dies, the spirit continues. All the world's great wisdom traditions acknowledge this.

It is a bit more complicated to think about this when a person dies in 1920 and as a spirit today still believes it is 1920 even though I am recording their actions and voices in the present day. The spirit apparently can see me but genuinely believes he is in 1920. That spirit has traveled backward in time; the evidence is that we could exhume his grave and find his remains today.

If I am accessing that spirit in a time he believes to be 1920—because he can *see* the physical trappings of 1920 all around him—I have accessed the spirit's world, but not in a way that allows me to see what the spirit is seeing. The physical world around me is still the present day. Thus, if I can travel forward in time because I am dead, I can also return to the period I came from. I can move backward and forward. Some theories present UFOs and aliens as our future selves coming back in time and doing exactly what I've described. Whether these entities are a future version of us or beings from another galaxy is too complex a topic for this book, but it is theoretically possible.

Time traveling aliens probably have presented to humans a range of vehicles during the period since they first visited us, but not necessarily in chronological order. Their first visit to Earth may have been yesterday, but they could then go back and visit us a millennium ago in the same vehicle. We may be looking up into the night's sky and see a Model T Ford sharing the same space as a Toyota Prius. Roger Kvande discusses this concept in the book *Extraterrestrial Odyssey*:

> The aliens, who according to Roger Kvande have time travel ability, allegedly can come into our times in an order different from our 'linear' time!

Linear History and Time Travel

Diagram A represents the chronological linear life of a person who died in 1920. It also shows key events in their life such as being born and starting work. If we access this person as a spirit in the present, the spirit is time traveling between its present, past and future. The person who died and became a spirit died in 1920 but haunts the period they believe to be 1875. They are having a dialogue with me in the present (such a clever ghost!).

If the spirit of a dead person wants to be in 1875, then by using the idea discussed in UFO travel, they should be able to project themselves into that time period. They also could then access the present by the same process, such as responding to my request for them to "come through" or by their need to watch over loved ones or relay a message.

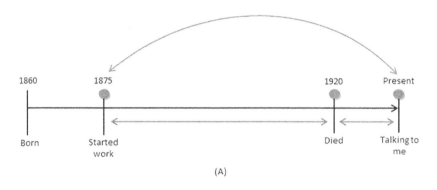

(A)

In the case documented in the book *Extraterrestrial Odyssey,* we learned that an abducted child needed knowledge of the planet Mars to direct the craft there. Is knowledge of a destination a necessary prerequisite to traveling there? Is travel then limited to destination that one has knowledge of? Apparently, you have to know where you want to go before you can go there. Contemporary quantum theory suggests nothing exists until we have a conscious knowledge of it.

A ghost, then, would have to know the location in which it wants to appear in order to show up there. This may answer why ghosts and spirits appear trapped in one location or are rarely seen outside of the environments they haunt—especially if the buildings around that haunted location are destroyed or redeveloped. If the only building left in town was built in 1862, then anyone in spirit who died before 1862 would be unable to haunt that lonely building. Those in spirit who died after 1862 would need to have obtained knowledge of that building during their lifetime in order to haunt it.

This may be why contact with ghosts from periods before the eighteenth century are rare. Spirits before that time could have no knowledge of the more recent structures of contemporary society.

Ghosts of English Kings and Queens are only able to haunt ancient castles because those ancient castles still exist, and the royal figures who are now in spirit once resided in those castles and remember them.

This theory also answers the question of why we never see the ghosts of cavemen. When you consider that we have been roaming the planet as humans for hundreds of thousands of years, shouldn't the spirits of those distant ancestors appear as ghosts everywhere? Well, there were no structures for those spirits to have knowledge of, thus no places to haunt except, perhaps, a few caves.

You Have to Know the Building

An example of having to know a building before you can haunt it appeared at the Maxfield House in Mankato, Minnesota. I held a vigil in the basement, and the spirit of George Maxfield came through via the ghost box.

"Why are you here?" I inquired.

"Legacy, legacy," George told me.

"So are you are here because this is the only property left for you to be in—the only building you remember that is still here?"

"That's pretty much it, yes."

This brief exchange also suggests that aliens must be looking at our sun and solar system in the same way we look up at Alpha Centauri. To be able to visit us they must be aware of us.

Aliens Copy Ghosts

If ghosts can think themselves into a place or situation and can physically interact with their new surroundings, could vast intelligences in other parts of the universe harness such a phenomenon, perhaps with the aid of a suitable machine or craft? Ghosts are naturally occurring, but aliens may have artificially copied and created *modus operandi* of the spirit world. This plagiarism is common within our own evolution and called biomimicry, the process of copying scientifically what nature has demonstrated.

There are many examples of biomimicry. In 1941, the Swiss engineer Georges de Mestral picked at burrs that caught on his clothing and his dog's fur. He placed a burr under a microscope and noticed it had tiny barbs that allowed it to attach to passing creatures. By copying the concept of the burrs, he created Velcro, a material that uses tiny barbs as a fastening device.

Gecko Tape uses nanoscopic hairs to cling to sheer surfaces, inspired by the hairs mimicked from the feet of geckos. Scientists hope to create an entire suit made of this material. This would allow the wearer to scale walls and even walk across ceilings.

The cataglyphis is an ant found in the Sahara Desert. Unlike other ants, the cataglyphis does not rely on pheromone trails to navigate through the environment. Scientists believe the ants use a combination of visual piloting, path integration, and systematic search to find their way. Engineers hope that by studying these creatures they can build robots with similar capabilities.

Use of Energy

In physics, the law of conservation of energy states that the total energy of an isolated system remains constant and conserved over time. This law means that energy cannot be created or destroyed; it can only be transformed from one form to another. We are alive and have electrical energy running through our bodies. So what happens to the electricity that allows us to move, our brains to function, and our hearts to beat after we die?

When a person dies, the energy in their body goes where all organisms' energy goes after death—into the environment. Energy stored in the body transfers into the animals that eat us—wild animals, if left unburied. When we eat dead plants and animals, we are consuming their energy and converting it for our own use. Worms, bacteria, and plants ingest and absorb a buried corpse. During cremation the energy converts into heat and light.

Paranormal investigators can detect an electrical field in which ghosts manifest themselves as physical entities. There are numerous devices available that register this anomaly, from EMF K2 meters to Melmeters. Ghosts produce readable energy, retain energy, and can absorb energy from the environment around them. As a qualified Reiki Master, I can deliver healing energy for the benefit of my clients. Nurses and care workers can also receive training in the skill of healing touch. I believe energy can imprint itself into the fabric of a building using the walls and floors like sponges for both negative and positive energy. As a psychic, I can sense if a traumatic incident has taken place at a location. Examples include my experiences while visiting European Second World War concentration camps and historic battlefields.

On a smaller scale you may have experienced a similar feeling. I have walked into a room moments after two individuals were having an intense argument and felt that the energy in that space was off, even without knowing what had taken place moments earlier. The energy of the negative interaction before my arrival was impressed into the environment. This is why you should never argue in the bedroom, a place best preserved for relaxation and sleeping.

UFOs Creating Energy

Ted Phillips asked my opinion on a case he was researching when we met at a MUFON conference in Minneapolis. Phillips is the Director of the Center for Physical Trace Research. He began investigating UFO reports in 1964 and was a research associate of Dr. J. Allen Hynek from 1968 until Hynek's death in 1986. Phillips began specializing in the physical traces associated with UFO sightings in 1968 and delivered presentations at the first International UFO Congress and MUFON symposium. Most recently he was a part of the History Channel documentary "UFO Hunters and Alien Encounters."

Phillips was researching an incident in which a UFO landed close to a factory. After the encounter, many of the factory workers witnessed ghosts and paranormal activity, refusing to come to work. The building had no history of paranormal activity before the UFO incident. Phillips wanted my views on the phenomena. I attributed the paranormal activity to the UFO leaving energy behind after its presence—*juicing up* the surroundings by default and allowing ghosts to benefit and manifest.

I believe EMF energy is how ghosts manifest themselves physically. Documented and recorded levels of EMF are often gathered with sightings. An electromagnetic field is a physical field produced by electrically charged objects. EMF extends indefinitely throughout space and is one of the four fundamental forces along with gravity, weak interaction, and strong interaction. If a heavily charged UFO interacted with a geographical location, it would leave that area open to a greater likelihood of paranormal activity.

Ghosts and spirits are energy. Energy is required to emit light in the form of an orb or to manifest physically. In Janis Amatuzio's 2008 book *Beyond Knowing*, she describes a light appearing in the corner of the room and getting brighter after someone died. Some believe this is a dead person coming back to visit. Energy is also required to slam doors, turn on lights and faucets, throw objects and instigate other stereotypical ghost-like behavior. During a walkthrough of the Windom Public Library in Cottonwood County, Minnesota, the team started the investigation by conducting a series of baseline tests. Within seconds of entering the children's library a book flew from the top shelf of the central bookcase and landed in front us. I wondered if a spirit was demanding our attention to open up communication. My team had rarely experienced such a prominent use of physical energy by the spirit world.

High EMF Readings in Long Prairie

Energy is measurable, and the paranormal investigator has tools and meters to record all kinds of energy from Electromagnetic Field meters (EMF) to static meters. These tools work in conjunction with ghost sightings and contact.

In 2016, I twice investigated a closed bank building in Long Prairie, Minnesota. As the team made its way along a corridor in the basement next to the vault, we noticed that a K2 EMF meter was spiking into the red with a measurement of twenty-five milligauss—the highest possible reading for this device. It stayed in this position for several minutes before disappearing, then randomly returned to this reading after a short interlude. I brought a second K2 meter into the area and recorded the same reading on this device. I believe a spirit was following us around as we conducted a walkthrough. This would explain the transient nature of the EMF readings. This building was currently unoccupied, and no other electrical equipment was present in the vicinity to contaminate my readings.

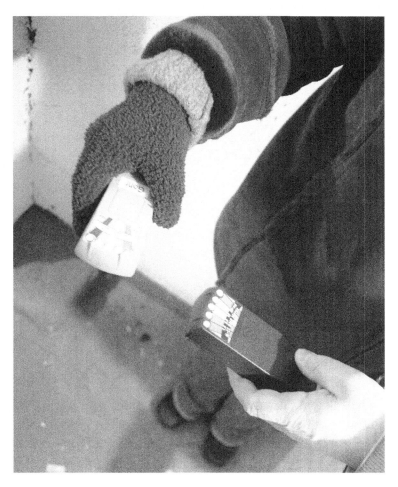

High EMF readings in the First National Bank in Long Prairie, Minnesota.

The Transfer of Energy

I believe the transfer of energy from a UFO to a specific location could be possible based on my own experiences and encounters. Ufologist Eve F. Lorgen, MA, proposes that aliens can harvest human energy in her article "Scavengers of Passion":

The hypothesis is that the aliens (at least certain species, including the Greys, Reptilians and Draconians) harvest human emotional energy, specifically the primal creative energy exuded during a high drama romantic obsession.

Lorgen continues by stating that some aliens see our energy as a delicacy:

According to the abductee, the White beings told her the energy we humans generate is a delicacy to them.

Lorgen suggests that aliens artificially create a romantic bond and "twin flame" scenario between couples so they can use the energy this creates:

Non-tangible energy fields refers to soul energy manifestations transmitted between persons who have deep connections to one another, consisting of subtle energies which can be sensed by clairvoyants.

The aliens harvest human emotional energy, specifically the primal creative energy exuded during a high drama romantic obsession.

Aliens Using EMF to Control

Nadine Lalich is a writer and abductee who believes aliens use EMF to control humans. Lalich co-authored the book *Alien Experiences* and published the essay "Alien Machines" in the *Journal of Abduction Encounter Research*. She describes a tunneling UFO that generated EMF energy to control the surrounding human population:

Fully extended and secured in the ground, the massive object spun rapidly in the cavern it had created, generating some kind of electro-magnetic energy the ETs implied was capable of physically affecting all the human beings living in the adjacent city. Thus I was informed that their ability to control us was not just through individual-to-individual telepathy or mind scan practices.

We can see energy transfer replicated in natural situations like lightning, for example. If aliens need to artificially replicate the ghost's ability to jump energy from one place to another using a machine, it could be similar to a Van De Graaf generator. I use an EM pump device to artificially flood rooms I am investigating with EMF in the hope of generating a catalyst for paranormal activity.

Transfer of Energy in Pipestone

Paranormal residual energy can attach itself to objects. I believe this is like the way a UFO can transfer energy into the surrounding area. In the incident reported below, we recorded the amassing of energy linked to physical contact with an entity.

The investigation took place at the Historical Museum in Pipestone, Minnesota, in 2013. Before our team starts any investigation the owner or manager usually gives us a guided tour of the property. During the walkthrough of the Historical Museum, an investigator made his way to the racked uniforms at the back of the textiles room. He ran a K2 meter along the uniforms to see if any energy had attached to them. The meter started to peak, reaching a high reading of twenty-five milligauss and illuminating the dimly lit room with a red glow. As the investigator distanced the meter from the uniforms in a controlled manner, the reading subsided. When he moved the device back into the proximity of the uniforms, the meter peaked again, suggesting that the uniforms were the source of the anomaly.

As the investigator moved the meter to the farthest part of the room an unseen force pushed his hand down. Whatever energy was emanating from the uniforms had made its presence known and wanted my investigator to stop. We reviewed the recording of the incident in the command trailer, and the footage clearly showed that his arm had been forcibly pushed downward.

With the volume turned up all the way, we reviewed the incident several times. Moments before the investigator's hand had been grabbed by the unseen force, we could clearly hear a distinct buildup of noise, a low-pitched hum that gained in volume during the seconds before the hand was pushed down. Then the hum quickly ceased as if it had grounded or discharged in some way. The noise reminded me of the way Fiona described the audio and ambient sensations in her bedroom moments before an alien arrived next to her in bed.

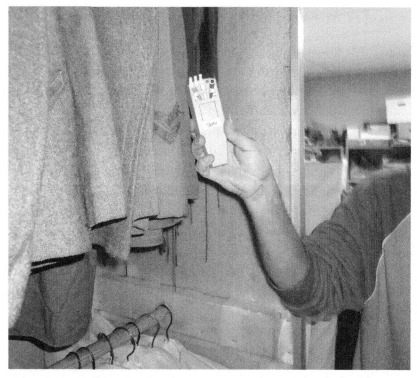

EMF recorded in the textiles room of the Pipestone County Museum in Minnesota, moments before the investigator was grabbed.

Transferring Energy into the Surroundings

I believe it is possible to create an atmosphere for paranormal activity by imprinting the energy of human emotions into a location. I investigated "The London Dungeon" tourist attraction in South London in 2011. It's a wax exhibition of gory and macabre history comprised of themed tableaus and live actors. The exhibition was in what used to be wine cellars, and the torture equipment displayed were reproductions. There has never been a history of deaths and torture at this sight, and no reason for it to be paranormally rich, yet I found this property to be highly active.

I believe the thousands of visiting tourists bring fear and the anticipatory energy of being scared—the attraction is a glorified haunted house where actors jump out of dark corners. Energy created through the action of collective fear may be imprinted there.

Energy at the Soap Factory

The Soap Factory building is the oldest unconverted warehouse space on the Minneapolis riverfront. Built in 1883, this cavernous cathedral of industrial space sits uniquely in the middle of the old milling district of the Marcy-Holmes neighborhood next to the Pillsbury Mill.

The whole paranormal team thought there was something very odd and disconcerting about the Soap Factory building. I believe collective negative thought created this energy. This is known as a *thoughtform*, or a *tulpa* in Tibetan mysticism. The word *tulpa* derives from the Sanskrit for "to construct" or "to build." The energy manifests consciously or unconsciously through sheer willpower alone. It is a materialized thought that takes a physical form.

The Soap Factory generates revenue from turning the basement into a haunted house experience during the Halloween period. This creates the added expectation of being shocked and scared on a collective level and generates an atmosphere of fear within the building throughout the month of October. It is possible this environment could be a catalyst for empowering anything negative already in the building, or anything transient attracted to the projected negativity.

Inside the Soap Factory in Minneapolis, Minnesota.

Human Energy Recorded

Dr. William Collinge documented experiments in his 1998 book *Subtle Energy: Awakening to the Unseen Forces in Our Lives.* Experimenting with two individuals, he was able to record electrocardiogram data from one person's heart and brainwave energy that was somehow present on the surface of the second person's body when the two were holding hands. On repeating the experiment with the subjects wearing latex gloves, the signal was still present but was only one-tenth as strong. The transfer of heart energy was recorded when the subjects were sitting three feet away from each other. Electrocardiogram output was also detectable across the space between them on the surface of each other's body. The scientific community has yet to verify these findings.

Orbs

UFO reports regularly record manifestations of energy as orbs. I started this book by discussing the foo fighters witnessed during the Second World War. Experienced ufologist John Carpenter believes orbs witnessed on a ranch in Missouri were extraterrestrial in nature and highlighted this in his article "Accepting the weirdness coming through dimensional openings: Hunt for the Skinwalker pulls it all together." Carpenter described witnessing blue orbs displaying intelligent maneuvering and red orbs that seemed to pay close attention to his livestock:

> Orbs of Light—other than the blue spheres which flew intelligently and seem purposeful.

One example is small, red, golf-ball size orbs that harassed animals on the ranch.

It is unclear whether the orbs witnessed were UFOs in the sense of vehicles or were the aliens themselves. An anonymous author, with a lifetime of experiencing his own abductions, published an article entitled "One man's struggle for freedom from abduction, has this abductee found a way to stop the aliens from taking him?" He stated that aliens can look like orbs of light when moving around an abductee's bedroom.

Have you ever seen floating balls of light? Would you like to witness floating balls of light in your bedroom? If so, then stay awake. It's an experience you won't regret. These floating balls of light come in red and white and each has an intricate pattern that reminds me of a crop circle or a computer chip. The white balls are about the size of a saucer, and the red ones the size of a silver dollar. I have witnessed these many times, as close as three feet away, and every time I see the beings in this form I am blown away. In my experience, once these balls of light move toward the window, they briefly glow as if alive (as of course, they are) and promptly disappear. They have gone through the window. Almost immediately there are bright flashes of light outside my window. How many flashes depends on how many aliens were in my house. I believe each ball of light indicates one Grey, just in case you were wondering. I have seen the Greys in several forms, but this is by far my favorite.

This account is remarkable in describing aliens using the same method of travel as ghosts and spirits. The ability to pass through physical barriers and appear like orbs of energy is positively paranormal. It leads me to wonder just how many paranormal orb sightings have actually been extraterrestrial in nature. It also suggests that aliens have harnessed the same mode of movement as ghosts, perhaps through biomimicry.

When a Ghost Turns Out to be an Alien

Bill Konkolesky is a UFO writer and state director for Michigan MUFON. In his article "The power of hypnotic recall: A skeptic is converted," Konkolesky described the childhood experience of seeing a paranormal floating skull at the end of his bed. He has attributed this phenomenon to extraterrestrial contact:

> Two of my four brothers also had strange experiences at that house in which we all grew up, and the family agreed the house probably had a ghost. (My other two brothers claim nothing unusual has ever happened to them.) I think my family probably believed me and likely thought I was visited by the "household ghost." As time went on there were several more "ghostly" encounters, and on my 17th birthday I received Whitley Strieber's *Communion* as a present in 1988. It made me question the "haunted house" theory. So much of what had happened to me fit eerily well into the category of UFO abduction phenomena.

Early UFOs Mistaken for Apparitions

Ghostly manifestations often reveal themselves to be like many UFO reports. The French philosopher C.J. Ducasse documented a case in his book *A Critical Examination of the Belief in Life After Death* in 1961. He quoted from a book written by Reverend Abraham Cummings entitled *Immortality Proved by Testimony of Sense* in 1826, in which Cummings experienced the apparition of a deceased woman he assumed to be a hoax:

> Sometime in July 1806, in the evening, I was informed by two persons that they had just seen the spectre in the field. About ten minutes after, I went out, not to see a miracle for I believed they had been mistaken. Looking toward an eminence twelve rods distance from the house, I saw there as I supposed, one of the white rocks. This confirmed my opinion of their spectre, and I paid no attention to it. Three minutes after, I accidentally looked in the same direction, and the white rock was in the air; its form a complete globe, with a tincture of red and its diameter about two feet. Fully satisfied that this was nothing ordinary I went toward it for more accurate examination. While my eye was constantly upon it, I went on for four or five steps, when it came to me from the distance of eleven rods, as quick as lightning, and instantly assumed a personal form with a female dress, but did not appear taller than a girl seven years old. While I looked upon her, I said in my mind "you are not tall enough for the woman who has so frequently appeared among us!" Immediately she grew up as large and tall as I considered that woman to be. Now she appeared glorious. On her head was the representation of the sun diffusing the luminous,

rectilinear rays every way around. Through the rays
I saw the personal form and the woman's dress.

According to Cummings this apparition appeared many times,
speaking and delivering discourses that were sometimes over an
hour long. In his pamphlet on the subject, he produced some thirty
affidavits from persons who had witnessed the apparition. Each time,
the manifestation had begun as a small luminous cloud that grew
until it took the form of the deceased woman. Witnesses observed
the form vanish in a similar manner. These experiences represent
one of the first documented UFO and ghost encounters in America.

Paranormal School Orb

During an investigation at an abandoned school building in Morton,
Minnesota, my team witnessed a bright, white orb traveling
intelligently through the furnace room in the basement. It was
admitting its own intermittent light as it flew just below the ceiling
and was recorded by the team. A series of photographs shows the
orb displaying different levels of illumination.

The moment an orb appears in the furnace room of the Morton
School in Renville County, Minnesota.

A close up of the orb.

An Orb at Hotel Francois

I investigated the building that was once the 19th century Hotel Francois in Redwood Falls, Minnesota. It is now used as a location for a Halloween haunted house attraction to raise money for local charities. The hotel has a history of deaths including a nasty strychnine poisoning in 1896. During paranormal contact in the basement, team leader Scott saw a rocking chair moving by itself in a creepy doll themed room, he then captured a long oval orb over the chair using a full-spectrum camera.

An oval orb over the rocking chair taken with a full-spectrum camera (photography by Scott Kenner).

EMF Used to Deliver a Message at the Canby Theatre

When a measurement of energy from a spirit is detectable on a device, it allows me to engage with the spirit using a basic dialogue. On an investigation, spirits sometimes approach the meters to register their presence. This can generate *yes* or *no* responses as the cooperating spirit moves in and out of range. The basement of the Canby Theater, Canby, Minnesota, provided an excellent example of this phenomenon.

A shadow figure walked along the basement corridor then stopped, stood in the doorway and looked directly at me. The K2 meter started to dance with an array of green and amber lights that blinked and flashed. I asked the entity to continue to illuminate the lights if he or she was male. The reading remained constant. After a minute I asked the spirit to keep the lights flashing if she were female. The lights stopped. I felt a coldness enter the room indicating the spirit had now joined us. I believe the previous action influencing the K2 meter had signified a male presence.

Using Energy to Communicate

I believe spirits can control energy, as I witnessed in the Christie House in Long Prairie, Minnesota. When conducting a vigil in the parlor, I tried to re-create the sound of a 1915 Edison Victrola. I believed this sound could be a catalyst for attracting the attention of any spirits that might be present. I've witnessed many positive results when implementing this technique in other historical buildings. In some early Minnesotan theaters, I have played the sound of period organ music that accompanied the live action of an old silent movie. The concept of trying to encourage spirits to respond by playing music from a certain period is called the "Singapore Theory," also known as the "Theory of Familiarization or Paranormal Stimuli."

The concept involves re-creating the audio experience of a particular era, providing a comfortable and familiar environment in which the spirits would be willing to interact. This theory can also involve filling a building with historical furniture to re-create a period atmosphere as in a museum tableau or the historical décor of a bed and breakfast. Other techniques include deploying trigger objects from a certain era with period costumes for the team, or re-creating a traumatic or historic event. It is no surprise that reenactors in period costume are a catalyst for ghosts and spirits. I witnessed this phenomenon at Fort Snelling in Minnesota, when a ghost army from the eighteenth century encroached upon the parade ground occupied by actors re-creating a drill in period uniforms.

Before the Christie House investigation, I had recorded several music tracks onto a compact disc and packed a portable stereo with my equipment. As the vigil began, I pressed the play button and waited. The first track was the 1912 hit "By the Light of the Silvery Moon" sung by Ada Jones and accompanied by a male quartet featuring Billy Murray. The track started with the usual crackling, hissing and clicking that accompanies the beginning of most old gramophone records. The Victorian parlor filled with the sound and atmosphere of a bygone era.

The music elicited the response I had hoped for, and the K2 meter flickered into life. It started to pulse from a neutral green all the way up to amber (fifteen milligauss) and then back again, indicating paranormal activity. EMF activity caused by non-paranormal influences produces a constant reading—the electrical device that activates the reading is either on or off.

The pulsing of the meter then began to synchronize to the rhythm of the song. I placed two additional K2 meters on the floor and watched all three devices blink in unison to the beat of the song. I grabbed my full spectrum camera and recorded the entire experience.

As the song finished, a second tune began. I noticed a discernible decrease in the registered pulsing energy. I suspected that whatever spirit had caused the previous pulsing was not as pleased with the second track, so I played the first song again. The energy immediately increased, and the readings began to pulse again. This indicated that an intelligent perpetrator was able to distinguish between each track and respond accordingly.

The parlor of the Christie House in Long Prairie, Todd County, Minnesota.

Aliens Using EMF

Ufologist Michael Menkin believes that aliens also use EMF to facilitate communication. He outlined his theory in an article entitled "Report on alien abductions and the Thought Screen Helmet":

> Given my scientific orientation, I realized if information was going back and forth between minds, the process must have a basis in physical reality. Telepathy must be an electro-magnetic transmission, but I had no idea, and I still have no idea, exactly what kind of EM transmission it is. Nonetheless, I started looking for material that could be used to shield the brain from EM transmission, and I proceeded by trial and error.

Ghosts Can Die

Spirits are generally more active in areas that have the best environment for them to operate. Sites that naturally emit high levels of EMF can by default have the greatest number of paranormal occurrences and sightings. These would be locations with a high level of electrical circuits and cabling, like the backstage of theaters and mechanical rooms. My equipment case contains an EM pump that fills the surrounding space with electromagnetic fields that improve the environment for better contact. Spirits use energy provided to boost their abilities.

It's also possible to ground or "earth" a ghost to remove its existence. Energy dissipates when it changes from potential energy to kinetic energy. This normally happens because of friction, heat, light and noise. Consequently, a ghost can lose energy.

An example of this phenomenon occurred during an investigation at the back of the stage of the Wieting Theater in Toledo, Iowa. The theater had a history of hauntings by a ghost named Ella that had not been encountered for a number of years. Contact began shortly after I started the vigil and turned on the ghost box.

"Is Ella there?" I inquired.

"No!" a male voice said emphatically.

"Can you go and get her?"

"She's not here."

"Why is she not here?"

"Because she's dead!"

"So was she once here as a ghost then?" I asked.

"Yes."

"So she was once a ghost here, and then her spirit died so she can longer be here?"

"Yes!"

"So is it possible to die twice, once in life, and once again in spirit?"

"Yes," the voice said.

Through the ghost box, the spirit had suggested Ella had once haunted the Wieting Opera House and that historical sightings by staff and patrons alike may have been correct in their assumptions of seeing Ella. But could it be that Ella had now passed for a *second* time in spirit, so she was no longer able to haunt the theater?

Ella had died on May 23, 1933, so her reported after-death actions of throwing lightbulbs, walking around the stage and appearing in the fourth row of the theater had used up some of her energy, leaving just enough energy to haunt for only eighty-three years. This can explain why some spirits are shadow figures—they no longer possess the energy to fully manifest. Shadow figures or shadow people are dark silhouettes with human shapes and profiles that flicker in and out of one's peripheral vision. Therefore, paranormal activity in buildings can subside over a period of time and explains why we rarely make contact with a ghost from more than 150 years ago, despite humankind's residency on the planet for millions of years. If this were not the case, we would still see the manifestations of Neanderthals from six hundred thousand years ago.

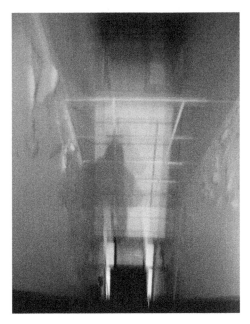

A hooded shadow figure in the entrance to
the Kemp Block Opera House.

Red Wing Rail Depot

I twice investigated the Red Wing rail depot in Minnesota during 2017. I developed such a good interaction with a female spirit on the ghost box that I eventually decided to ask more probing questions about what it means to be in spirit.

"Can you die in spirit?" I asked.

"Yes," she said.

"Where do you go when you die in spirit?"

"Home."

"So where is home?"

"Earth," she said.

"So when you die in spirit, you come back to Earth?"

"Yes!"

The Rail Depot in Red Wing, Minnesota.

This brief and very interesting interaction suggests the spirit believed herself to be beyond the vicinity of Earth in her current form, yet possessed the ability to interact with me in Red Wing on Earth. I believe they may have been suggesting they were on another plain or dimension, one that does not anchor them to Earth and the physicality of gravity and other terrestrial forces. It made me consider that the knowledge that makes us the individuals we are is stored in a place away from Earth, like a metaphoric hard drive of stored information somewhere in the universe.

The spirit said she would come back to Earth once she died in spirit. I believe dying in spirit is when energy has been exhausted and dissipated. Coming back to Earth after this occurrence suggests a form of reincarnation.

Shadow Figures Seen by Experiencers

In her book *Mosaic of the Extraterrestrial Experience*, November Hanson discussed the idea of experiencers becoming susceptible to seeing shadow figures and other paranormal phenomena after alien contact:

Oftentimes people who have had an extraterrestrial type experience have other types of experiences not necessarily related to being extraterrestrial in nature. I think we sort of lump all these experiences together and call them paranormal. Over the years I have heard people describe other types of events not necessarily related to the focus of this project. One I had heard of in the past was the sighting of shadow beings. These dark vestiges seem to be something that is noticed in the peripheral vision, at first creating an initial startled reaction that something has momentarily invaded one's environment.

Is it possible that being exposed to an extraterrestrial environment leaves us susceptible to experience other anomalous activities? I have often wondered if that were the case.

Christie House Shadow Figure

The Christie House in Long Prairie, Minnesota, is a great example of the Richardson Gothic style of architecture. Built in 1902, it was the home of Dr. George Christie who used it for a medical practice. During an investigation in 2014, I experienced physical paranormal activity, including high energy readings and a shadow figure in the same incident. The kitchen has a large, sturdy wooden table that served as an operating table for patients in the early nineteenth century. I believed the table might be holding some residual energy from the pain and anguish suffered during these operations.

In the doorway to the kitchen, I set up an IR video camera that covered the table and the laundry room beyond. I placed a selection of trigger objects on the table, including a large red and white fishing bobber and a coin, which I drew a circle around on a piece of paper to mark its exact position. I also placed an EMF K2 meter next to the objects, all in view of the camera. The area under constant observation was a controlled space with no access by any of the investigators.

I turned out the light, shut down the room and left the camera running for the duration of our time in the house. As we were setting up our first vigil in the parlor, the entire team heard the sound of the bobber bouncing around the floor in the kitchen. We hurried back to the controlled space and turned on the light. The bobber had moved to a place under the table. I was confident the incident had been captured on video.

We played the footage back instantly. On the monitor we watched a bizarre series of events unfold. Less than a minute after I had turned the light off, a large number of orbs started appearing in the darkness. One orb rocketed from the top right corner of the screen to the bottom left corner at high speed. Several orbs then shot through the kitchen and disappeared into the laundry room. Each of these orbs emitted light, and the autofocus on the camera struggled to focus on them as they appeared and disappeared.

Suddenly, a band of darkness moved across the room from left to right and swept back again. Seconds later, a slightly moving dark shadow, like one cast by a person, appeared on the door to the pantry. Then a bobber dropped off the table with a swirling orb dancing around it.

The Kitchen in the Christie House in Long Prairie, Minnesota.

Radiation and UFOs

Any vehicle arriving on Earth from outer space would bring with it energy in the form of radiation. The radiation in deep space is different from that on Earth's surface or in low-Earth orbit. It is unlike the x-rays and gamma rays we know. All material in space eventually becomes radioactive due to nuclear interactions with cosmic rays, radiation belt protons, and solar flare particles. Radiation-induced spacecraft anomalies were first recorded on the Explorer I launch on January 31, 1958, when a Geiger counter placed onboard suddenly stopped counting due to the saturation of high radiation. This led to the discovery of the Van Allen belts.

There are many examples of witnesses coming into contact with radiation. In physics, radiation is the emission or transmission of energy in the form of waves or particles through space or a material. There have been UFO encounters where the experiencer has received the empirical evidence of radiation burns. Radiated ground also provides measurable proof of UFO landing sites.

In 1980, a sighting called the Cash-Landrum incident occurred in the Piney Woods area of East Texas. The witnesses insisted the UFO contact was responsible for damaging their health and became one of the few cases that resulted in a civil court proceeding.

Betty Cash, Vickie Landrum and Colby Landrum left a restaurant around eight thirty p.m. Thirty minutes after driving along an isolated local highway, they noticed a bright UFO above the treetops. The craft straddled the road, blocking their way.

The UFO suddenly sent down an intermittent cone of fire like a rocket blast. The witnesses described the UFO as diamond shaped with a dull aluminum surface. It bleeped, had blue lights running around its center and lit up the forest like daylight. They got out of the car and felt the bright light burn their skin. A group of twenty-three helicopters, including several large, double-rotor CH-47 Chinooks, appeared and flew in erratic patterns before bunching around the UFO.

Over the next few hours, Betty's skin turned red, as if badly burnt by the sun. Her neck became swollen, and blisters erupted around her face, scalp and eyelids. She vomited throughout the night. By morning, her hair began to fall out, and her eyes became so swollen she was unable to see for a week. Then she entered into a coma.

Vickie and Colby suffered similar symptoms but to a lesser degree. Doctors believe that exposure to radiation caused these symptoms. Several other witnesses also saw the UFO that evening, including local residents and an off-duty police officer.

The Stefan Michalak Case

Another famous case involved the effects of radiation after UFO contact. The incident occurred on May 20, 1967, near Falcon Lake, Manitoba, Canada. Stefan Michalak was an amateur geologist and had left his motel at five thirty a.m. to explore a quartz vein he'd discovered near a marshy area.

At 12:15 p.m., he looked up and saw two cigar-shaped objects glowing red at an estimated altitude of forty-five degrees. As the objects descended, they appeared more disc shaped. The farthest of the pair stopped in mid-flight as the other one landed on a large flat rock 160 feet away. The first UFO hovered for a short time before it departed, changing from red to orange, then to grey, as it flew away into the west and disappeared.

The landed UFO turned from red to grey, then finally took on the appearance of stainless steel. Michalak observed the UFO for thirty minutes and even made sketches. It was saucer shaped, forty feet in diameter and at least ten feet deep. Its upper dome was an additional three feet high. Michalak felt waves of warm air radiating from the craft accompanied by a sulfurous smell. He also heard the whirring sound such as made by a motor and a hissing noise as if the vehicle were venting gases.

A three-foot door opened on the side of the craft revealing internal lights. Michalak approached within sixty feet of the craft and heard two humanlike voices, one with a higher pitch than the other. Michalak believed the craft was an American experimental vehicle and walked closer. Poking his head into the opening, he saw a maze of lights on what appeared to be a panel and noticed beams of light creating a horizontal and diagonal pattern. A cluster of computer-like lights flashed in random sequences.

As Michalak stepped away from the craft, three panels slid over the opening like a camera shutter to seal it. He then touched the outside of the vehicle with a gloved hand. There were no signs of welding or joints. The surface was highly polished like a colored glass that reflected the sunlight. He stood facing a grid-like exhaust vent nine inches high and six inches wide that contained a uniform pattern of round holes, each about one-sixth of an inch in diameter. A blast of hot gas suddenly shot from these holes into his chest, setting his shirt and undershirt on fire and causing severe pain. He tore off his burning garments and looked up just in time to watch the craft leave. He felt a rush of air as it ascended.

Michalak noticed the strong stench of burnt electrical circuits mixed with the smell of sulfur. He walked back to his belongings and noticed the needle on his compass spinning erratically. As he drove back to the motel, he began to feel nauseated and broke out in a cold sweat. Moments later he was overtaken by weakness and dizziness. He vomited several times and developed a severe headache.

More than a dozen doctors examined Michalak. They all diagnosed radiation burns and other physiological effects. Ground traces at the landing site recorded radioactivity and mysterious metal fragments.

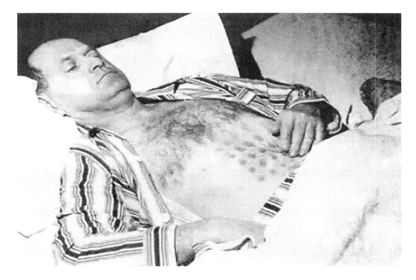

Stefan Michalak recovering in hospital with radiation burns
clearly visible on his stomach.

Other UFO Energy Phenomena

Incidents of UFOs interfering with energy and electrical circuitry
are quite common. In 1965, James Townsend encountered a silver-
finned rocket standing forty feet high on a road outside Long Prairie,
Minnesota. It affected the electrical systems in his car and shut down
his engine.

On November 2, 1957, a frightened man called the sheriff's
office to report that a two–hundred-foot rocket had lifted off from
a field and then rushed toward his truck in Levelland, West Texas.
As the craft flew overhead, the truck's engine died, and the lights
went out. An hour later, a second report also documented the same
phenomenon. That same night, Sheriff Weir Clem and a deputy also
made visual contact with the UFO. Ray Jones, the local fire marshal,
also experienced engine difficulties when he witnessed the same
UFO that evening.

Many witnesses have experienced an invisible force field that
stops experiencers when approaching UFOs. In the winter of 1967,

Claude Edwards tried to walk toward a UFO that had landed in his Missouri cow field. An invisible force field stopped him within fifteen feet of the UFO, and he could not push beyond it.

UFOs and Power Plants

The effective use of EM pumps during paranormal investigations suggests that spirits can absorb energy from the environment. I believe a spirit could access an electrical substation and use it as a catalyst for manifestation. My experience of interacting with ghosts and spirits in electrical rooms and near electrical theatre equipment has demonstrated this. My own blue sphere sighting south of Willmar also suggested the vehicle was interacting with nearby wind turbines. Other UFO sightings have also been reported around power plants and other facilities that generate energy.

On January 3, 2015, the director of a French nuclear power plant in Nogent-sur-Seine, southeast of Paris, reported a UFO sighting over the facility. According to European news agencies, UFOs flew over nuclear power plants in France on eighteen separate occasions between early October and early November 2014. In late November, France's secretary-general of defense and national security (SGDSN) posted a press release on the issue:

> Although currently listed overflights do not present
> a threat jeopardizing the proper functioning and
> security of nuclear facilities, they are nevertheless
> a warning about potential risks from inappropriate
> or malicious use.

According to the French newspaper *Sud Ouest*, a director from one of the nuclear power plants expressed his opinion that it was not a drone but a UFO that had flown over the complex. Pascal Pezzani, director of the Blayais Nuclear Power Plant in southwestern France, held a presentation on the plant's results for 2014 and the outlook for the plant in the future. Pezzani addressed the drone issue and stated:

Here, we have not seen a drone. We saw a UFO,
and there was no impact on the safety of our sites.
Our position is clear.

A declassified government document released by the Nuclear
Regulatory Commission (NRC) described a triangular shaped UFO
that hovered above a nuclear power plant for two consecutive nights.
An unnamed officer who worked at the Cooper Nuclear Station near
Brownville, Nebraska, gave this description:

> An unidentified flying (UFO) object violated the
> protected area at Cooper Nuclear Station between
> 1986 and 1989, but the event was not reported
> to the NRC as required. The CI (confidential
> informant) described an event that occurred during
> his employment as a security officer. He was
> employed there from 1986 through 1989 and did
> not remember specifically when during that time
> the event occurred. While posted at the intake
> structure one night, he observed an "unidentified
> flying object" fly down the Missouri River about
> 150 feet in the air and hover in front of the intake. He
> observed it for a few moments and then contacted a
> fellow security officer who also observed it.

The pair watched the UFO together as it went back up the
river. When they reported the incident, colleagues did not believe
them. The following evening, the officer saw the UFO return and
hover just north of the reactor building. The witness described it as
triangular with a rotating circle of lights on the bottom. It was silent
and one-third the size of the reactor building. They alerted security
officers at the plant who also witnessed the UFO.

A Vortex

A presentation on energy would not be complete without discussing
a vortex, which is a concentrated area of high electromagnetic energy

that can be permanent or temporary. French scientist, mathematician and philosopher René Descartes studied vortex theory and proposed that in a vortex cosmic energy rotates around a central point or axis. From the beginning of the mid-nineteenth century, the word *vortex* has meant any whirling movement of energy or particles.

Two photographs show a Minnesota resident entering
her house and capture a vortex by accident.

Vortices are doorways to other dimensions or planes. Thus, non-human entities and spirits may be able to access Earth by accessing them. In one sense, they are highways to other places not of this world. The frequency and placement of vortices are based upon Earth's own EMF and the position of naturally occurring geographical features, which act as catalysts.

Today it's common to send information over fixed microwaves and fiber optic cables. If an alien or ghost is pure information, then it can travel from point A to point B using energy as the vehicle.

A vortex can appear in photographs as white, opaque streaks and lines running through the picture in paranormally active locations. On occasion, a vortex can look like elongated ovals or even look like braided cable or rope. Some people use this term "vortex" to explain lines or narrow cylinders that appear highlighted in ghost photos. In 2013, a Minnesota resident sent me two photographs of her parents arriving home after a shopping trip. Clearly, a cable type vortex is visible in the photographs.

Photographs are notoriously unreliable sources of evidence, however. I have seen double exposures taken on digital cameras and flashes reflected and bounced around to create all kinds of false positives. Digital cameras also fire a beam of light to the targeted object to measure the distance from the camera so the proper focus can be set. This beam occasionally is captured in photographs as a colored anomaly. Use caution and diligence when identifying a vortex based solely on photographic evidence. The photographs presented here show stronger evidence than most because the photographer took two pictures, and the vortex anomaly appears in both showing movement. In my experience, cold spots, anomalies in EMF readings, and an increased chance of paranormal contact accompany vortexes.

Shared Olfactory Experiences

Paranormal activity and UFO encounters can share the phenomenon of sulfurous smells. Demonic entities and the presence of spirits have always been associated with the odor of sulfur, but UFOs can also produce this stench. The Stefan Michalak encounter previously presented is a good example. I believe there is a connection between sulfurous odors and the high discharge of energy.

Electrical Discharge

Benjamin Franklin's first experiments with lightning led him to describe a sulfurous smell in the notes he forwarded to the Royal Society in London. Russian born scholar Immanuel Velikovsky stated that an electrical discharge passed through air creates sulfur, although he theorized an enormous amount of energy would be required to transmute sulfur from oxygen.

If lightning creates sulfurous smells, it should be no surprise that the two are complementary to one another in mythology when describing the retribution of the Gods. The link between discharges of lightning combined with foul-smelling sulfur links fire and brimstone to the judgement of God in Biblical times, for example, in the story of Sodom and Gomorrah. Historical Greek literature also links sulfur with deity activity in Homer's twelfth book of *The Odyssey*:

> Zeus thundered and hurled his bolt upon the ship
> and she quivered from stem to stern, smitten by the
> bolt of Zeus, and was filled with sulfurous smoke.

Homer continues this theme in the *Iliad*:

> [Zeus] thundered horribly and dashed it to the
> ground in front of the horses of Diomedes, and
> a ghastly blaze of flaming sulfur shot up and the
> horses, terrified, both cringed away against the
> chariot.

Entities require energy to be physical or to manifest themselves. It would be reasonable to believe that energy passing through the air could create the sulfurous smells encountered on paranormal investigations.

The Old Jail House

The Old Jail House in Taylors Falls, Minnesota, is now a bed and breakfast. I experienced the phenomenon of sulfurous smells during a vigil in the building. The odor lingered for several minutes before dissipating. It was a rotting smell with no obvious source. I wondered if this could be a residual olfactory haunting that transcended the centuries. The site previously was a jail house so the smell could have come from a time when a toilet bucket existed in the cramped, poorly ventilated cell during a hot Minnesota summer. The owners had never experienced this foul odor before... or since.

UFOs and Sulfurous Smells

It may be possible that when an entity travels between two dimensions to our time period, the accompanying sulfurous smells could travel with it. This could explain previous encounters with similar smells during periods of high activity. Sulfurous smells have been reported with close craft sightings of UFOs, so we can reasonably assume the UFOs are generating large amounts of energy that ionizes the surrounding atmosphere to create sulfurous smells.

In the book *UFO Dossier* by Kevin Randall, a witness of a UFO encounter from August 29, 1967, described smelling sulfurous odors. Creature sightings from September 12, 1952 in Flatwoods, Kentucky and from August 24, 2005, in Indianapolis, Indiana also reported strong sulfurous odors. Many abductees have reported these smells when taken onboard UFOs, which has contributed to an association between demonic entities and aliens in people of a religious mindset.

Alien's Smell

Derrel Sims's first abduction from his bedroom in Midland, Texas, happened when he was a small child in 1952. In the *Journal of Abduction Encounter Research*, under the title "One kid who didn't buy it," he recalled the olfactory experience of having an alien appear in his room:

> He had a strange faint smell. It smelled awful...

Psychic Smells

Sensitives can often obtain psychic knowledge by means of smell. This ability is referred to as clairolfaction, clairescence, or clairalience, literally meaning *clear-smelling*. My experience in Taylors Falls was not a psychic phenomenon, though—the smell was not limited to me but was present in the room for all to experience. There is a distinction between physical and psychic detection of an odor.

I have experienced a psychic olfactory sensation on many occasions. During an investigation in a room at the Sweet's Hotel in Le Roy, Minnesota, I recognized the smell of funerary lilies. On a vigil in the Kemp Block Opera House in Long Prairie, Minnesota, I was informed of what the room had originally looked like by smelling of heavy cigar smoke hanging densely below the high ceiling. I also recognized the smell of male body odor when a spirit arrived in the Corner Drug Store building in Sauk Centre.

Atmospheric Conditions

Earth's atmosphere naturally creates energy. Static electrical fields occur in fair weather and under thunderclouds. Friction can also separate positive and negative charges and generate strong static electric fields. In daily life, we may experience spark discharges with grounded objects or hair rising as a result of friction when walking on a carpet or taking off a sweater. The use of DC electricity is another source of static electric fields. It is used in rail systems, televisions and computer screens with cathode ray tubes. If UFOs harness naturally occurring weather conditions or influence weather conditions, we should experience sightings of UFOs in poor weather.

Bad Weather UFO

The Green Bay Packers quarterback Aaron Rodgers described seeing a UFO during bad weather in 2016:

> It was a large, orange, left-to-right-moving object. Because of the overcast nature of the night and the snow, you couldn't make out... it was behind the clouds we were seeing, but it was definitively large, moving from left to right. And it goes out of sight, and we look at each other and go... "What in the f— was that?"

In 2018, I interviewed a woman named Debs from Sacred Heart, Minnesota, who saw a UFO during a severe rainstorm. She described and sketched her experience. The famous Roswell incident in 1947 occurred during a thunderstorm. But the reporting of UFO sightings in poor weather is not complete enough to be meaningful. Many MUFON field reporters leave descriptions of weather, and historical cases are hard to find. During any form of severe weather, the likelihood of witnesses being out in the elements and looking at the skies is poor, and reduced visibility makes the useful sighting rare. Still, as described, such sightings do exist.

Aliens Effect Air Pressure

Elaine Douglass describes the experiences of abductee Jim Sparks in the *Journal for Abduction Research*. Douglass's article, called "The breaking of Jim Sparks, or why the aliens don't land on the White House lawn," describes how his abductors manipulated the air pressure to control Jim Sparks:

> The air pressure in the room changed. It pushed against my head and my ears, quite painful. My heart pounded again. I could taste fear again— body fear, fear of more pain that might come. Everything tightened... this discomfort would continue unless I cooperated, unless I drew the alien A on the screen. Still, I said, "No!" The air pressure increased, upping my discomfort and anxiety. Unless I obeyed, it would go up again. But I was still angry. "No!" I said, "I won't do it." But I could bear only so much. After the next level of agony, I cried out "I don't want to die!" and I wrote the alien letter on the screen. Instantly the air pressure dropped. My heart rate fell, and the anxiety and fear faded. Moreover, I felt euphoric. A very pleasant sensation flooded me.

Paranormal Air Pressure Changes

I have often recorded air pressure changes during paranormal activity. A device called an EDI measures changes in EMF, ambient temperature, motion, vibration, humidity and air pressure. During a 2017 basement investigation of the Rail Depot in Red Wing, Minnesota, I recorded a sudden change of air pressure and temperature when sighting a shadow figure, accompanied by a loud thump. During this contact, I also registered a spike in EMF, and several motion detectors acknowledged movement.

I also witnessed a change in air pressure and EMF fluctuations when a fishing bobber trigger object fell to the floor of the Volstead House in Granite Falls, Minnesota, in 2018. During this poltergeist phenomenon, I also experienced shadow figure activity.

Ghosts and Atmospheric Pressure

Air pressure is the weight exerted by the air around us directly related to its temperature and altitude. Even the smallest changes in pressure can affect us physically. The nerve endings on our joints have receptors that sense pressure changes and can respond with pain. Headaches can occur, and even the regularity of births and sperm counts alter noticeably. These physical changes are so subtle that our brains may not consciously recognize the shifts in our bodily functions even though we may unconsciously sense that some change has happened.

Changes in barometric pressure directly affect the amount of oxygen in our body. Higher pressure will generate more oxygen than lower pressure. The blood vessels in our brain contract and expand to regulate the amount of blood flow required in any given area to compensate for the variation in oxygen levels. This regulatory process and subsequent change of blood flow can result in neuropathic pain that can vary from a mild headache to more intense pressure headaches or migraines. Anti-inflammatory pain-relief drugs work by reducing the inflammation of the blood vessels.

Changes in air pressure can also cause the human body to have problems with mobility. Joints are vulnerable to these changes because the fluid and tissue surrounding a joint may become inflamed. Paranormal activity triggers changes in atmospheric pressure, and due to the subsequent physical changes in our bodies we can sense when activity is imminent. This may explain why we inherently appear to sense if a building is haunted.

Paranormal activity creates a pressure change by developing cold spots. A sharp drop in temperature creates high pressure, which causes an increase of ions, which are often associated with paranormal activity. There is also a shift in the ratio of positive and negative ions in the air during a thunderstorm. If hot air rises and cold, denser air sinks down from the roof, the two masses of air may meet at some point in a building. If that point happens to be the fifth floor, for example, then the meeting of the two pressures would create a micro atmosphere, which would generate moisture and ions—perfect conditions for ghosts and spirits. Thus, the fifth floor may be more haunted than the third floor because the conditions there favor the possibility of a haunting.

Entities manifesting on the fifth floor may then harness the static energy available to them in the air the same way they drain my team's batteries and power supplies. In old buildings with less climate control, pockets of perfect conditions are created throughout the interior by the confluence of low and high pressures. This may explain why newer buildings appear less active paranormally. Certain floors or rooms in buildings are labeled active because that is where perfect conditions exist.

Damp and humid atmospheres enhance the conditions for activity by altering the way electrical energy dissipates into the environment. Think about it—you are more likely to be shocked by static electricity in dry conditions. Wet environments also provide less resistance and create higher currents. If the coldest, wettest environments provide the best conditions for ghosts to manifest, it could be that graveyards, basements and castles are traditionally the best (and consequently the most stereotypical) locations for hauntings.

How Is It Possible

If I interact with a ghost in 2019 that died in 1920 but is haunting in what it believes is 1875, we are either jumping around in time, or we may all be going down the same path together, but our contacts are converging at those moments of time. The latter concept would be like different dimensions converging in one place at the same time. November Hansen discussed this concept in her book *Mosaic of the Extraterrestrial Experience*:

> If I understand the whole space time thing correctly, time in the 4th dimension is happening on a variety of axes, and we have been briefly removed from our own linear time and exposed to a different time environment. In my way of thinking this would explain the variations of time experienced.

Linear History

The task for any historian is to place all the data and facts into an easily accessible form that the reader can understand. If you write about a historical figure, the easiest framework for that work is to put the information in chronological order starting with the figure's birth and ending with their death. This framework is fine for the simple presentations but presents an unrealistic view of what time could be—as shown in Figure I.

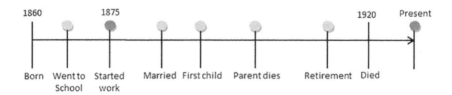

Fig. I

The chronological model does not work well from the perspective of the historian. If the subject was a famous artist like Vincent Van Gogh, for example, what would happen to the historian's text if a painting produced in 1885 was suddenly found to have been painted ten years earlier? The rigid chronological model would disintegrate. I can apply this model of linear history to the contact I have experienced with ghosts and UFOs.

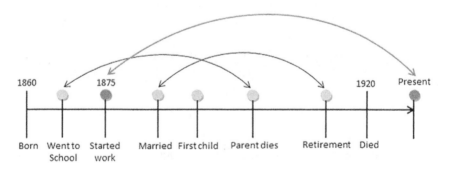

Fig. II

Figure II shows the linear model of travel between the future, present and past. I am in the present, but I am interacting with a ghost that believes it is 1875, the year that spirit first started work. The spirit has chosen to think itself into this timeframe and has chosen to create the exact surroundings it recalled from 1875. To the spirit, the current year may as well be 1875. Yet the spirit died in 1920. For me to have an interaction with that spirit, I must either go back in time to join that spirit, or the spirit must have go forward in time to join me. If the spirit goes forward to a point long after it had died (representing travel into the future), the spirit and I have converged in the same place. This suggests a spirit could create for itself any time period from its memory and can travel to it, either backward or forward, along its own linear line of history. If the spirit decides to think itself into the year 1880 when they married, it can do so, and I can access the spirit in 1880 from my point in the present.

The memories of the spirit I believe are stored knowledge the spirit can access in its mind. Obviously a spirit does not have a physical brain, but its mind must still be operable. The spirit and I are like two radios receiving the same broadcast—but the radios are in two different eras. The environment around the spirit that makes it 1880 is based on collectively pooled knowledge derived from every human that ever experienced that room, not just the recollections of the individual whose spirit is haunting it. This is like doing an image search of the Oval Office in the Whitehouse and re-creating a composite from the thousands of pictures available. Every sentient being capable of thought has produced a quantum hologram from information seen and experienced of an individual, place, or object. Those holograms must be transmitted, stored and made accessible. The spirit that is creating that composite image doesn't need direct knowledge of a building or place to haunt it, but someone must have gained a knowledge or memory of it. A spirit cannot visit or haunt a place that no one has ever seen or experienced.

The linear chronological model is familiar but does not reflect the idea that we are all in the same place at the same time. The linear model has us jump backward or forward in time whenever I believe I am in the same timeframe as the spirits. What is required from a useful model is to place all our time periods together in one place—our contact with the past in the form of a ghost, and also from the future, with all contacts taking place in the present. All of these periods in history and the future must converge into the present for us to access them and have contact.

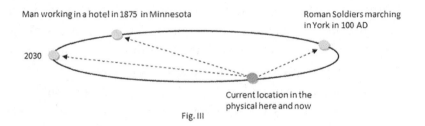

Fig. III

This model (Figure III) has three periods of history all happening at the same time but in different places.

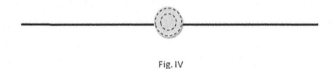

Fig. IV

If the spheres overlap with the present (Figure IV), I can access those eras, allowing me to have a dialogue with an individual from those periods if they wish.

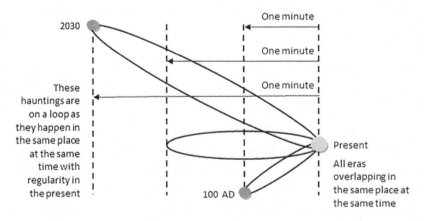

Time could move at different speeds for ghosts in the future and past compared to our present

Fig. V

(Figure V) represents the same concept, but the other eras are on different planes and dimensions than our own. Still, we can see where we would overlap and be able to access those times when making contact. This model also represents how other planes may have different references of passing time and can explain the idea of residual (looped) hauntings, such as making contact during the anniversaries of an event. This model illustrates the other planes and shows how time can move differently in each plane.

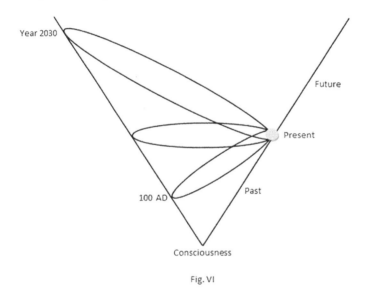

Fig. VI

It can also show (Figure VI) the expansion of knowledge from the first moment of consciousness. Figure VI is useful because it shows how time is altered during contact with spirits or aliens.

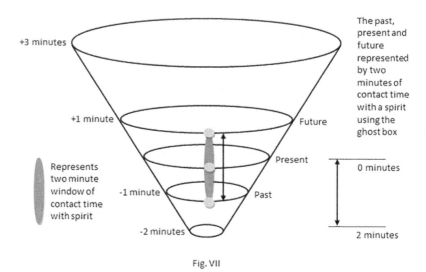

Fig. VII

Figure VII represents two minutes of contact time with a spirit. It shows how we can gain time during an interaction with a spirit or alien from another plane if the process steps outside of our own linear time structure. It illustrates how two minutes of real time can feel like three minutes during a contact. Time warping that occurs when our eras overlap in the same place is shown back in Figure VI.

Time is moving forward constantly during contact time; it is not static. Even as you read this sentence, your act of reading has already become history and the next sentence will be in the future— until you read each syllable in the here and now.

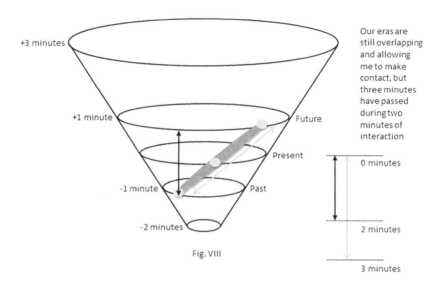

Our eras are still overlapping and allowing me to make contact, but three minutes have passed during two minutes of interaction

Fig. VIII

Figure VIII highlights how we can keep the present (the contact time) moving along and still overlap the era we have accessed because time is passing for me, so it must also be passing for the spirit I have accessed. It may not be in the same time increments as myself, but my two minutes of conversation has used up their time as well.

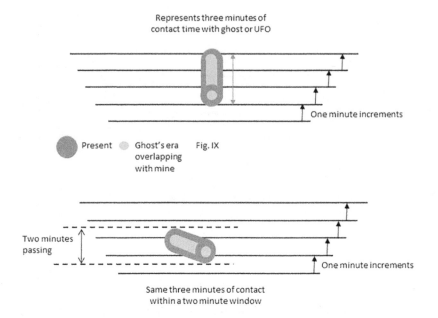

Represents three minutes of
contact time with ghost or UFO

One minute increments

Present   Ghost's era   Fig. IX
            overlapping
            with mine

Two minutes
passing

One minute increments

Same three minutes of contact
within a two minute window

Figure IX shows how the entire body of knowledge of all living creatures since the dawn of time can exist on a flat disc and could be stored like a giant hard drive for access by our minds and other creatures outside our own solar system. This hypothesis is taken from the study of quantum theory, which I address in following chapters.

The Redwood Falls Incident

Many of the concepts discussed in this book came together in one remarkable UFO encounter I witnessed on July 1, 2017. I reported this sighting and presented the empirical evidence to MUFON the following day. Two experienced field investigators documented the incident as case number 84799. The opening of this book outlined the way ufologists share the same equipment as the paranormal investigator. The UFO contact I experienced was important due to the measurable scientific data I recorded with my paranormal devices and tools. The contact also illustrated an erratic flight pattern and recorded measurable energy.

I conducted this paranormal investigation with my team at the Redwood Falls Cemetery in Redwood County—latitude 44.55121, longitude -95.09957. The team contained six professionals—two government workers, two doctors and two authors. It was a clear evening with perfect visibility and no cloud cover. I recorded a temperature of 67°F/19°C with no abnormal weather conditions. The flight path to Minneapolis MSP airport was twenty miles south, and we could clearly see aircraft on that path with navigational lights and marker beacons.

We stood respectfully around the grave of a deceased woman with whom we hoped to make paranormal contact. I had previously asked her about her history to solve a period crime. On this evening I placed several scientific devices around the site in order to record empirical evidence. At 10:20 p.m. I started the vigil by asking the spirit if she was present and willing to talk.

At 10:30 p.m. I asked an investigator to register our precise location using a GPS device and compass. We discovered the compass to be inoperable; it was locked in one set position. The GPS device also malfunctioned. This indicated a high source of magnetic interference and a jammed GPS satellite signal. The two different EMF meters I placed around the grave suddenly spiked into the highest reading of twenty-five milligauss indicating the arrival of a large, readable electromagnetic charge. The static meter indicated a high reading of static electricity at the same moment. The ghost box radio scanner began pulsing with a loud hum that faded in and out. It was a sound this device had never produced before. Every tool had been functioning perfectly before this incident.

I inspected the malfunctioning ghost box.

We looked up to see a large, yellow fireball moving slowly across the sky, brightly emitting a fluctuating, flame-like light. We watched the fireball speed up, slow down, hover, drop altitude and fly very erratically. This aerial display lasted for five minutes before the fireball continued its horizontal path from east to west until it was out of sight. The object was large and about ten thousand feet away traveling at three to four hundred mph with no noise. According to the Minnesota flight map, no recognized flight path exists for that area of the sky and the direction it flew. The entire team remained calm as it scientifically recorded the encounter on a digital video recorder in night vision mode, narrated commentary on several digital voice recorders and made extensive notes.

Five minutes after returning to the vigil, a second UFO appeared in the same part of the sky. This one was red and orange with a similar flame-like quality. Its flight pattern mirrored the erratic movements of the first UFO for the same length of time. Again our equipment registered anomalous readings for electromagnetic fields, static and audio. This encounter finished in the same way as the first one, with the UFO disappearing into the west.

Then, at the same interval as the first two sightings, a third UFO appeared with a similar yellow flame as the first and followed the same erratic flight path for the same length of time. The total contact time for the three UFOs was nearly a half hour.

This was an important and historic encounter for many reasons:
- It was a prolonged contact of twenty-five minutes.
- Six credible and experienced individuals witnessed the encounter.
- It left measurable empirical data from many devices in real time.
- It was a contemporary, not a retrospective investigation.
- It was a multiple sighting of three UFOs.
- The UFOs exhibited erratic flight patterns.
- Digital equipment recorded the encounter visually and audibly.
- There were perfect atmospheric conditions.

This encounter gave me firsthand experience to prove my hypotheses, much preferred over analyzing secondary accounts. It also strengthened my theory on the methods by which UFOs create and share the same readable trace evidence as ghosts. It is rare to investigate a UFO encounter as it is happening and not through historical accounts.

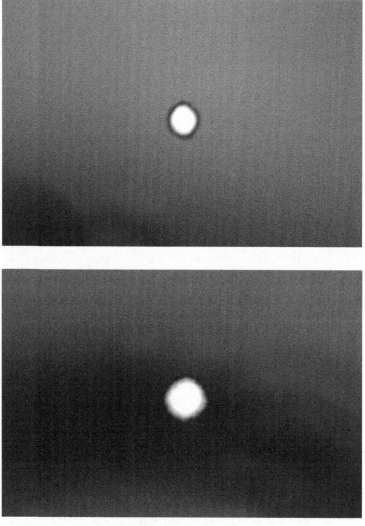

The first UFO sighting at Redwood Falls—a screen shot taken from the video camera in night vision mode.

The Nature of Consciousness in Psychology

As a historian, I am compelled to discover and analyze facts. Using historical records, which provide contemporaneously gathered and reported facts, I can verify material I gather from spirits, proving the reality of the many encounters I have reported throughout this book.

I am certain the information I receive during psychic readings from the dead is genuine and correct. I always provide my clients with pages of accurate, detailed notes about the deceased—information I could not possibly know through any other means. Normally my clients are strangers when they approach me. During investigations, I receive memories and details from psychic conversations with the deceased and then provide the client with knowledge long since forgotten. Being the receiver of information from spirits means that the information they reveal to me must be stored somewhere in a transmittable form.

My psychic abilities also allow me to read people's intentions and thoughts. This means I am able to connect with everybody, dead or alive, on an invisible level. This also includes animals, as obtaining a basic understanding of their thoughts is achievable. I have performed Reiki healing on many horses and dogs, psychically sensing their thoughts and feelings. I can also hold an inanimate object and gain knowledge from it. In other words, everything living, dead, or inanimate can transmit information.If aliens could also access this invisible knowledge, our thoughts, memories, and experiences, in the same way I can with clients, the deceased, animals and objects, it would allow them to have an understanding of where we are and what we are. Their sentient UFOs could then use this knowledge to come and find us. If a higher being, God for example, also accesses the same information, it would explain answered prayers and provide an explanation for miracles, if that higher being is proactive in responding to our thoughts and wishes.

I Perform Reiki Healing on horses.

If all this knowledge and information is storable it would explain ghosts and hauntings. The information of who that person once was is available with all their thoughts and memories and is accessible to the psychic, as demonstrated in my books, which contain a wealth of material provided by the dead.

Remarkably, an explanation for everything I have just presented is provided by two fields of study—psychology and quantum physics. Swiss psychologist Karl Gustav Jung and other prominent thinkers and philosophers of the last century believed that a collective consciousness exists throughout the universe. Contemporary quantum physics provides a scientific hypothesis to further explain Jung's ideas.

Quantum physics can explain a natural phenomenon that has been validated in the laboratory. This explanation is based on the mathematical theories of how nature implements and utilizes information, memory, perception, attention and intention. Quantum physics can explain many phenomena in nature for which no answers were previously available. This is particularly useful in accounting for the transfer of information between material objects, or between objects and their environment.

Quantum physics offers both a hypothesis and evidence to explain how living terrestrial organisms know and utilize information. In doing so, it elevates the concept of "information" to the same universal status as "matter" and "energy." Quantum physics describes the universe as a self-organizing, interconnected, conscious, holistic system.

Let me explain how science deals with solid, visible, quantifiable matter—and how anything invisible like ghosts and the transmission of thoughts are generally considered not "real."

Psychology and Consciousness

In the last century, scientists considered physics and psychology to be unrelated, yet both of these scientific disciplines led to revolutionary changes in the Western understanding of the cosmic order. They separately discovered a non-empirical realm of the universe that does not consist of material things, but rather of forms. These forms are "real" even though they are invisible because they have the potential to appear in the empirical world and act within it.

When French philosopher René Descartes declared that the world consisted of two kinds of material—thinking substance and extended substance—and when physicist Isaac Newton declared that "God in the beginning formed matter in solid, massy, hard, impenetrable, moveable particles... so very hard, as never to wear or break in pieces," Western science became materialistic. Anything that wasn't matter didn't matter.

Naturalist Charles Darwin introduced Newton's materialism

into biology. In his theory of evolution, having or not having stuff became the essence of life. Greed and aggression became the natural virtues of society segregating one individual from the next, one country from another, and one species from all others. In this view, the classical world was a segregated world. The physical sciences had nothing to do with ethics, philosophy had nothing to do with the arts, and the order of the universe had nothing to do with the way in which we should live. French biochemist Jacques Monod described this in his book *Chance and Necessity*:

> Man must at last wake out of his millenary dream and discover his total solitude, his fundamental isolation. He must realize that, like a gypsy, he lives on the boundary of an alien world; a world that is deaf to his music, and as indifferent to his hopes as it is to his suffering or his crimes.

In this totalitarian and materialistic environment, psychologist Carl Gustav Jung had the courage to propose that our minds are guided by a system of real, powerful forms called archetypes that are invisible and without mass or energy. In his book *The Archetypes and the Collective Unconscious: Volume 9*, Jung described the archetypes as a "psychic system of a collective, universal, and impersonal nature." Out of this system the invisible forms can appear in our mind and then guide "our imagination, perception, and thinking."

As it turns out, Carl Jung's revolutionary views of the human mind are in perfect agreement with the discoveries of quantum physics. The quantum phenomena now force us to think that the basis of the material world is non-material and that there is a realm of the world that we cannot see because it does not consist of material things, but of non-material forms. These forms are real, even though they are invisible because they have the potential to appear in the empirical world and to act on us. The forms in the cosmic potentiality are thought-like patterns of information that hang together like the thoughts in our mind. The world now appears to be an undivided wholeness in which all things and people are interconnected and consciousness is a cosmic property.

Jung Provides Answers

Jung's analytical psychology leads us to the conclusion that there is a part of the world that we can't see, a realm of reality that doesn't consist of material things but of non-material forms. These forms are real even though they are invisible because they have the potential to appear in our mind and act in it. This view is in complete contrast to our previous experience of the world. It derives from Austrian physicist Erwin Schrödinger's quantum mechanics, which is currently the only theory that allows us to understand the properties of atoms and molecules.

In this theory, the electrons in atoms and molecules aren't tiny little balls of matter but are standing waves or forms. All atoms consist of positively charged nuclei, which contain most of the mass of the atom, and of electrons, which are arranged in the space surrounding the nuclei. Electrons are tiny elementary particles. They have a definite mass, and whenever we see one, it appears as a tiny dot—a flash on a TV screen, or a little mark on a photographic film. In contrast to their appearances, the electrons in atoms and molecules aren't tiny material particles that run around the atomic nuclei like planets around the sun. They are standing waves. When an electron enters an atom, it ceases to be a material particle and becomes a wave. German physicist Max Born discovered that the electrons in atoms are probability fields.

Probabilities are dimensionless ratios of numbers. They carry no mass or energy, just information about numerical relationships. Yet the visible order of the world is determined by the interference of these waves. The interferences of atomic wave patterns determine what kind of molecules can form, and the interferences of molecular wave forms determine how molecules interact. For example, the molecules in your body interact in such a way as to keep you alive.

The order of the visible world, then, is a phenomenon that transcends the materialism of classical physics. If one pursues the nature of matter to the level of atoms and molecules, one finds oneself in a realm of mathematical forms and numbers in which all matter is lost. Therefore, the basis of reality is nonmaterial.

The Wholeness of the Physical Reality

Quantum physics raises the issue of the wholeness of the physical reality. By the concept of wholeness, we mean that seemingly separated things are connected and can act instantaneously on each other over long distances. In a holistic universe, decisions made by an observer in one part of the world can have an instantaneous effect on the outcome of processes somewhere else a long distance away. For example, a thought that appears in my mind at this moment may instantly appear in your thinking in another part of the world. This is nonlocality, meaning that two particles, which at one time interacted but have moved away from one another, can stay connected and act as if they are one thing no matter how far apart they are.

In classical physics, an action taken in one part of the world can have an effect somewhere else after a delay during which the signal travels from one point to the other. In the quantum world, the situation is different. Influences can act instantaneously over long distances, even from one end of the universe to the other.

The wholeness of reality refers to the connection between the wave properties of elementary particles. The metamorphosis of particles to waves, and waves to particles, is a general phenomenon that not only describes the modes of existence of electrons, but is a characteristic of all elementary particles—atoms and molecules. Whenever we see an elementary particle, it appears as a tiny material thing at a specific position in space. In contrast, when an elementary particle is on its own, like in a vacuum, it ceases to be a material particle and becomes a wave. You can think of this process as a spontaneous transition of a particle from its particle state to a wave state.

Greek physicist Menas Kafatos and American English professor Robert Nadeau describe the holistic nature of reality in their book *The Conscious Universe*. They argue that if the universe is an indivisible wholeness, everything comes out of this wholeness and everything belongs to it, including our own consciousness. Thus, consciousness is a cosmic property. This quantum view of a holistic reality is in perfect agreement with one of Jung's most important ideas, the archetypal idea of Unus Mundus—one world, as described in his book *Mysterium Coniunctionis, Volume 14*:

> Undoubtedly the idea of the Unus Mundus is founded on the assumption that the multiplicity of the empirical world rests on an underlying unity, and that not two or more fundamentally different worlds exist side by side or are mingled with one another. Rather, everything divided and different belongs to one and the same world, which is not the world of sense.

Individuation and Searching for Wholeness

The process of individuation is an innate capacity of the individual to become aware of the Self. Robert K.C. Forman, former professor of religion at City University, New York, describes this innate capacity in all of us, which is an imperative, life-long process of transformation. It is an impulse to unite what is divided. In *The Archetypes and the Collective Unconscious,* Jung affirms that:

> I use the term "individuation" to denote the process by which a person becomes a psychological "individual," that is, a separate, indivisible unity or "whole."

Searching for wholeness would be meaningless in a Newtonian world of separate material things. In the quantum world, it has found a physical basis. Jung understood the process of individuation as a religious impulse, which is a wholesome spiritual archetype that directs and coordinates the flow of human life. The word "religious" is used in this context to mean *reconnect, to be in bond* or to *reunite.* Swiss analyst Anniela Jaffé states:

> Individuation must be understood in religious language as the realization of the "godly" in the human, as the fulfilling of a "godly mission." The conscious experience of life becomes a religious experience... one could just as well say, a mystical experience.

In agreement with the aspects of wholeness that appear in the quantum view of the universe, Jung believed that the psyche has a natural and innate urge toward wholeness. Jungian analyst Joseph L. Henderson pointed this out in the book *Ancient Myths and Modern Man*:

> A sense of completeness is achieved through a union of the consciousness with the unconscious contents of the mind. Out of this union arises what Jung called "the transcendent function of the psyche," by which a man can achieve his highest goal: the full realization of the potential of his individual Self.

The craving for wholeness is the real opus that underlies all of Jung's work. In accordance with quantum physics, the meaning and purpose of our nature is anchored in the numinous realm of reality. Jung describes this spiritual quest this way:

> The main interest of my work is not concerned with the treatment of neurosis, but rather with the approach to the numinous. But the fact is that the approach to the numinous is the real therapy, and inasmuch as you attain to the numinous experience, you are released from the curse of pathology. Even the very disease takes on a numinous character.

Consciousness in the Universe

In the 1930s, British astrophysicist Sir Arthur Stanley Eddington was one of the first physicists who systematically searched for aspects of consciousness in the universe. He concluded in his book *The Philosophy of Physical Science* that:

> The universe is of the nature of a thought or sensation in a universal Mind.

Eddington suggested that when physicists make measurements their observations make sense because the measuring instruments connect with a meaningful background of the objects that are measured. For example, when we observe the movement of a light dot through the sky at night, our observations make sense because we know the planetary background in which the planets revolve about the sun. In this situation, Eddington pointed out, observations of atoms are a problem because their background is unknown. Whenever we see an atom, we can see phenomena that occur at its surface, but we don't know what happens inside. The electrons in atoms are nonmaterial forms, so their background is unknown. Science has nothing to say about the building blocks of the invisible world.

A similar situation arises in neurology. No measurements of the surface of a brain can tell us what is going on in the mind. Behind the surface of a brain there is a mind and a person who can tell what is going on in this mind. Atoms do not have people who live inside them that can tell us what is going on behind the surface. Eddington suggested that we should think of the brain and the atom together. He concluded that atoms are mind-like and have thought, as described in his book *The Nature of the Physical World*:

> Why not then attach it to something of spiritual nature of which a prominent characteristic is thought. It seems rather silly to prefer to attach it to something of a so-called "concrete" nature

inconsistent with thought, and then to wonder where the thought comes from.

To Eddington, the unity of the universe makes it necessary to conclude that behind all empirical appearances of the world "there is a background continuous with the background of the brain." Unity in this context means coherence. The universe is a coherent system based on the unity of our mind, Eddington proposes in his book *The Nature of the Physical World*:

> If the unity of a man's consciousness is not an illusion, there must be some corresponding unity in the relations of the mind-stuff, which is behind the visible surface of things.

Thus, from our own inner sense of unity, we can infer the unity of the world. If the universe wasn't a coherent system, but instead a random collection of disconnected piles of material debris, the unity of our thinking would merely be an illusion. On the other hand, if the universe is a coherent whole, the existence of our personal mind suggests that the background of the universe is mind-like. Because of this, Eddington concluded:

> The universe is of the nature of "a thought or sensation in a universal Mind"... To put the conclusions crudely—the stuff of the world is mind-stuff. As is often the way with crude statements, I shall have to explain that by "mind" I do not here exactly mean mind and by "stuff" I do not at all mean stuff. Still this is as near as we can get to the idea in a simple phrase.

Quantum Wave Functions are Archetypes

It is no accident that the development of psychology as a science took a huge leap after 1900 when the era of classical sciences came to an end and the quantum era began. Jung's view of the human psyche presupposes a structure of the universe that is in perfect agreement with the quantum universe but is impossible in Newton's world, in which all phenomena depend on the properties of matter.

Jung's "collective unconscious" is a non-personal part of the human psyche. It is a realm of forms—the *archetypes*—that can appear spontaneously in our consciousness and act within it, influencing our imagination, perception, and thinking. The archetypes are "typical modes of apprehension" that shape, regulate and motivate the conscious forms in our mind the same way virtual states of atoms and molecules shape and control empirical phenomena. We must constantly reach into the realm of the archetypes and make use of their virtual forms to truly be alive and give meaning to life.

Guiding the Evolution of Life

Molecules are guided in their actions by the wave forms of their quantum states; in other words, they are influenced by inner images. Since these inner images control all the processes of the world, they must have guided the evolution of life. As a result, biological evolution is not an adaptation of life forms to their environment, but the adaptation of minds to increasingly complex forms— archetypes—in the cosmic potentiality.

In our minds, cosmic forms appear as thoughts. We understand the world because the forms within our mind, and the structures of the world outside our mind, both derive from the same cosmic source. It makes sense, then, to believe that all of reality is like the reality of the atoms. That is, behind the visible surface of things there is a realm of invisible forms that have the potential to appear in the empirical world and act within it. This is like waves that are bound together mind-like, indivisible whole—the ocean. Thus, the universe exists as an indivisible wholeness, and consciousness is a cosmic property. The appearance of the archetypes in our minds shows our connection with a transpersonal order beyond the narrow confines of our personal psyche. Jung described the collective unconscious in *The Archetypes and the Collective Unconscious, Volume 9*:

> A boundless expanse full of unprecedented uncertainty, with apparently no inside and no outside, no above and no below, no here and no there, no mine and no thine, no good and no bad... where I am indivisibly this and that; where I experience the other in myself and the other-than-myself experiences me... There I am utterly one with the world, so much a part of it that I forget all too easily who I really am.

Mystics and idealist philosophers have pursued such ideas through the ages. In the nineteenth century, Georg Wilhelm Friedrich Hegel taught that "Absolute Spirit" is the primary structure of the universe. Everything that exists is the actualization of spirit, and everything is connected with it. Spirit is everything, creates everything, and everything is one. Thus, Hegel concluded, our thinking is the thinking of the Cosmic Spirit, who is thinking in us.

Synchronicity and the Mind-like Background of the Universe

In Jung's theories the concept of synchronicity plays an important role. Jung used the phrase "coincidence according to meaning." This describes the phenomenon that occurs when two or more events are connected in meaning but not in their visible causes and something other than chance is involved. This is called synchronicity, and it consists of two factors: first, an unconscious image that comes into consciousness either directly (literally) or indirectly (symbolized or suggested) in the form of a dream, idea, or premonition; and then an objective situation that coincides with this content.

When someone dreams of an unusual event, and the next day that same event actually occurs in another part of the world, the dream and the event have produced a case of synchronicity. In the dream descry bed above, an inner mental state coincides with an external event that takes place outside the observer's field of perception at a distance only verifiable afterward. In classical physics, coincidences related by meaning are impossible as non-random events, so they must be random. Classical physics does not allow for physical phenomena that are causally connected and don't involve the exchange of physical energy or forces.

Quantum physics suggests that reality appears to us in two domains. There is the domain of empirical, energetic and material things—the world of the actuality of the visible phenomena. There is also a domain behind the visible one, a realm of the hidden, invisible and non-empirical. This second domain does not consist of things; it is non-material and non-empirical, the realm of the potentiality of the universe. As the visible world is the consciousness of the universe, the hidden world is the unconscious.

The non-empirical forms in the cosmic realm of potentiality are real because they have the potential to appear in the empirical world and act within it. They do this in two ways: as thoughts and images in our conscious mind; and as material structures and events in the external world. When they both appear at the same time—as a thought *and* as an external event—we experience synchronicity. In a Newtonian world, such events are impossible. In a quantum world, they *must* occur. We do not know what causes such events because their causes are non-empirical. However, we can understand that synchronistic events are possible because the universe is an indivisible wholeness that is aware of its processes—like a cosmic spirit. This goes back to Georg Hegel's thesis that a thinking cosmic spirit is in all of us.

Synchronicity can involve more than a single mind and more than a few events. In the early 1900s, Europe went through an era of revolutionary changes that affected all aspects of life and which showed all the characteristics of synchronistic events. In 1900, Sigmund Freud invented psychoanalysis; Max Planck founded quantum physics that same year. In 1903, Henry Ford founded the

Ford Motor Company; that same year the Wright Brothers succeeded in the first human motor flight, and just two years later Albert Einstein developed relativity theory. Beginning in 1905, within a span of just eight years, the first modern art show presented paintings by André Derain and Henri Matisse in Paris; within two years Georges Braque and Pablo Picasso developed Cubism; Arnold Schönberg wrote the first composition of atonal music; Wassily Kandinsky invented abstract painting; and Franz Kafka published his short stories. In 1914 James Joyce wrote *The Dubliners*, the First World War began, and 1917 saw the Russian Revolution. All of these developments were revolutions in their corresponding fields.

We perceive a synchronistic connection between these revolutions because they had common meaning. Each one of them in a given field away moved the visible surface of things into a hidden, abstract, and more fundamental realm of the world. For example, when quantum physicists discovered the non-empirical realm of the world, the painters of modern art began to search for the essence of things behind their visible surface, and psychologists discovered the hidden power of the unconscious.

German art historian Werner Haftmann explained in his book *Painting in the 20th Century* that paintings had become evocative and stopped being reproductive. When physicists abandoned the notion of the eternal point, like the particle in quantum physics, the visual abstract artists abandoned the infinite point of perspective, which was the cornerstone of all classical paintings.

There was little physical contact or direct communication between these various pioneers of the time. The physicists did not invent the phenomena of quantum physics by pondering the paintings of modern artists. Artists did not invent modern art by listening to atonal music. These different minds connected in the wholeness of the mind-like background of the cosmic potentiality. The cosmic spirit was at work in a synchronistic process.

The Nature of Consciousness in Quantum Theory

The quantum theory of consciousness presents a method of integrating traditional religious and esoteric views of the soul, afterlife, and the possibility of other realms of existence, with contemporary scientific theories on the relationships between consciousness and the body—between subjective perception and objective physical reality. It is the contemporary scientific hypothesis that provides the structure and mechanisms for Jung's thinking.

According to Jung's theory, our consciousness, or mind, exists as a self-aware energy containing information beyond our perceived three-dimensional reality and cosmos. Our body exists within the three-dimensional universe and receives the energy and its information as transmissions from the mind in the same way a radio receives radio signals from a broadcast station.

We experience these transmissions and signals as thoughts, feelings, mental images and other forms of mental activity. We experience our mental activity as occurring *within* our body, within some *internal* realm of experience, just as we seem to hear sound coming from within the radio as if it somehow *contains* all the music that comes out of it. However, just as the broadcast that comes out of the radio originates from a distant station, our thoughts and feelings—which seem to appear from inside our head—actually come from a transcendent realm in which our mind is located.

Most notably, the French philosopher and Nobel Laureate Henri Bergson proposed this alternative view of the relationship between mind and body as early as the nineteenth century. What's particularly interesting about this theory is it can accommodate the most cutting-edge experimental observations of neuroscience and quantum physics as well as the most contemporary and unbelievable aspects of religious teachings and paranormal activity.

If our brain is a radio sending and receiving information to a mind outside of space-time, then damage to the brain should allow observable corresponding damage to mental function, just as damage to a radio would interfere with its ability to receive signals and broadcast properly. However, killing the brain doesn't necessarily kill the mind, just as smashing a radio doesn't eliminate the broadcasts coming from the radio station.

Mainstream scientists typically say the brain creates consciousness and that consciousness cannot survive without the brain. But under the quantum theory of consciousness, one can argue that consciousness exists before the formation of the brain, therefore it can exist after the death of the brain. If a mind can exist after death in some form, we have a plausible explanation for ghosts.

We commonly believe the universe, an incalculably vast and complex chain of physical events, created consciousness, which is our self-aware thinking and feeling mind. But it might be that a preexisting consciousness or mind caused the creation of the universe.

A Scientific Model for Universal Consciousness

Many notable scientists, including Edgar D. Mitchell, Stephen Hawking, and Dr. Rudolph E. Schild, have promoted the study and theory of quantum holograms (QH), which provide a model for describing the basis for consciousness. QH explains how living organisms know and use whatever information they have access to. It elevates the role of information in nature to the same fundamental status as that of matter and energy. These and other scientists speculate that QH seems to be nature's vast, built-in mechanism for storing and retrieving information—one used since the beginning of time. QH can explain how the whole of creation learns, self-corrects, and evolves as self-organizing and interconnected.

The dictionary defines consciousness as "the ability to be aware of and to be able to perceive the relationship between oneself and one's environment." However, the most basic definition is simply "awareness." Other words used when referring to awareness in animals are thoughts, sensations, perceptions, moods, emotions, and dreams. Consciousness is easy to recognize, but difficult to define. At a basic level, consciousness is associated with a sense of separation and awareness of the surrounding environment from the conscious entity. It also seems to be associated with the ability to process, store, and act on information gathered from an external environment.

Consciousness is not restricted to a functioning brain, however. Microscopic organisms such as viruses, amoeba, and algae are conscious in a primitive sense. They do not have brains, a nervous system or neurons, yet they demonstrate purposeful behavior and are aware of their environment. An amoeba searches for food by surrounding, engulfing and digesting prey. Several types of algae change the process of how they obtain food based on available sunlight; when light is plentiful, they gravitate toward food, which they sense through a photoreceptor at one end of the cell. If the light is too bright, they will swim away to more suitable lighting conditions.

Many scientists do not consider viruses to be living entities because they do not meet their criteria for life. Viruses do, however, exhibit some aspects of consciousness, or at least some rudimentary form of an awareness of their surroundings. Unlike most organisms, viruses are not made of complete cells. They reproduce by invading and taking over the machinery of their target host cell. When a virus encounters a potential host, it inserts itself into the genetic material of the host's cell. The invaded cell is then instructed to produce more viral protein and genetic material instead of performing its normal functions. This demonstrates intentionality over purposeful behavior. Simple living entities are conscious to some degree since they display a level of awareness and intentionality to manipulate their environment.

Passing on Characteristics

For a long time, the primacy of DNA as the master blueprint for an organism has been the central dogma for biology. There is now very convincing evidence that all organisms on Earth, from plants to mammals, acquire characteristics through interaction with their environment and can then pass these characteristics on to their offspring, according to microbiologist Bruce Lipton. This process is called "epigenetic inheritance" and has spawned a new field in biology called epigenetics, which is the study of the mechanisms by which the environment influences cells and their offspring without changing genetic codes. This is forcing scientists to rethink evolutionary theory and return to the days of Lamarckian evolution. French biologist Lamarck developed a theory fifty years before Darwin and hypothesized that evolution was based on cooperative interaction between organisms and their environment. This interaction enabled these organisms to pass on adaptations necessary for survival as the environment changed.

Lipton stated that results from the Human Genome Project are forcing biologists to the recognition they can no longer use just genetics alone to explain why humans are at the top of the evolutionary ladder on earth. For example, there is not much difference in the total number of genes found in humans and those found in primitive organisms. So where does the information come from that defines who we are? Lipton wrote that cellular constituents are woven into a complex web of crosstalk, feedback and feedforward communication loops and that thousands of scientific studies over the years have consistently revealed that EM signaling affects every aspect of biological functioning. This is an interesting development based on a common characteristic of ghosts and UFOs—their use of EMF in readable amounts.

Inter-Cellular Communication

In addition to DNA and environmental influences in all Earth-based living organisms, inter-cellular communication is especially critical in embryonic development. From a single fertilized egg, the embryo divides thousands of times, each time producing identical offspring cells called stem cells. At some critical point when the embryo has reached a certain size, something truly miraculous happens. Cells begin to differentiate and form groups of like cells that will eventually become all the highly specialized tissues and organs that make up the human body. Out of the entire mass of undifferentiated cells making up the embryo, how does a particular stem cell suddenly know it is supposed to transform into a heart cell, liver cell, or neuron? Electrochemical signaling with the immediate surrounding cells provides some of the instruction for differentiation. This exchange is necessary and provides information about how a cell must change to become the right type of cell at the right place at the right time.

How an Organism is Created

Parapsychologist and biologist Rupert Sheldrake studied the problem of whether signaling by itself is sufficient to explain the full development of an embryo into a complete organism. He proposed a theory called the Hypothesis of Formative Causation that describes an alternative explanation for how the structure and form (morphology) of an organism develops. In his model, developing organisms are shaped by fields that exist within and around them. These fields contain the form and shape of the organism. He proposed that each species has its own information field, and within each organism there are fields nested within fields. All these fields, he suggested, contain information derived from previous expressions of the same kind of organisms.

He stated that a field's structure has a cumulative memory based on what has happened to the species in the past. This concept applies not only to living organisms, but also to protein molecules, crystals and atoms. In crystals, suggested theory states that a cumulative memory forms the shape and growth of the crystal.

If a field of memories exists, along with the information that defines the uniqueness of an individual, this has implications for paranormal activity if those fields can be stored in some way after the person has died or can be absorbed into an environment. A quantum hologram can exist without the physical body. This applies to all living species across the universe and may allow aliens to project that hologram into other solar systems or give a biomechanical UFO the ability to take the hologram's information stream and travel to another location with a crew inside.

Sheldrake's view is that nature forms habits and memories, and over time these habits strengthen and influence following generations. Similarly, other habits atrophy over time from lack of continued use. Sheldrake is not alone in proposing such a mechanism. The great psychologist Carl Jung has proposed "the collective unconscious" as previously discussed, which represents a vast information store containing the entire religious, spiritual and mythological experiences of the human species.

French philosopher Pierre Teilhard de Chardin proposed the concept of the "noosphere," which represents the collective consciousness of the human species that emerges from the interaction of human minds. De Chardin asserted that as the individual and global society evolve into more complex networks, the noosphere evolves along with it.

The Akashic record is a similar concept that developed in the Sanskrit and ancient Indian culture. It is described as an all-pervasive foundation that contains not only all knowledge of the human experience, but also the entire history of the universe. Our normal five senses cannot access this information, but it is available through spiritual practices such as meditation. Hungarian philosopher Ervin Laszlo has promoted a theory called the A-field, which contains many aspects similar to the previous concepts. All these ideas imply a mechanism similar to QH, and all propose a means for accessing transcendent information via the process of resonance.

Since the laws of nature appear to operate the same everywhere, there is no reason to believe that QH would not also apply to biological entities anywhere in the universe. In higher organisms with brains, the massively parallel-processing capabilities of the brain are capable of simultaneously resonating with QH information at an incredible range of frequencies. This is something I believe aliens have achieved.

Quantum Theory can Explain Psychic Communication

Science now believes consciousness begins with quantum events. Recent evidence suggests that certain quantum phenomena operate at the macro as well as the micro level and are responsible for many otherwise unexplainable phenomena that living entities experience (as described by physicist Ellery Schempp and ufologist and NASA astronaut Edgar Mitchell). This theoretically resolves how twins, or a mother and child, seem to communicate telepathically, how a ghost can communicate with a psychic, or an alien with an abductee.

The remote transfer of nonlocal information between humans is not difficult to understand—hundreds of successful experiments have established the case. In all these cases no energy transfer is required, only nonlocal information, as each person has access to his or her own energy source. The teleportation of quantum information has been successfully accomplished for particles, as described by Darling, and is used in practical applications for quantum computing.

Rupert Sheldrake conducted experiments with dogs in which the animals correctly anticipated their owner's departure from a remote location to return home. He also conducted other successful experiments on previously unexplained behaviors of animals. In one example, rats learning to traverse a maze benefited nonlocally from the experience of other rats that had previously learned the maze. Other examples include distant nonlocal awareness of deaths and accidents, animals that heal humans and sense forebodings of natural and manmade disasters.

We have all experienced a sense of foreboding without understanding why only to discover a relative or friend had died or been involved in an accident. It is common to think about an individual and then that person calls on the phone. Many people have reported being lost on a car journey and then gained a sense of the correct direction only to discover later it was the right course.

It is no surprise that humans exhibit an even wider range of reactions to nonlocal information than animals. The evidence suggests that humans can perceive, recognize and give meaning to nonlocal information across a broad range of complexity from inanimate objects to simple organisms, animals and other humans. The existence of QH provides a theoretical model for making sense of observed results that repeatedly fall outside of the prevailing paradigm.

Consider the case of an infant separated from its parents during a time of war or disaster. Years later, by a chance reunion, the now unfamiliar child and birth mother sense a strong connection while others do not. This feeling of connectedness is due to the resonance between the mother and child during pregnancy and through the birth process.

Evidence suggests that the brain and mind have such capabilities at birth. Unfortunately, these consciously intuitive perceptions atrophy quickly due to the development of language, cultural conditioning and the subsequent lack of practice. Perhaps cultural conditioning is one of the reasons why so-called reincarnation experiences are common in children of eastern cultures while virtually unheard of in the west. Dr. Ian Stevenson of the Department of Psychiatric Medicine at the University of Virginia traveled around the world and investigated children from age two to five who claimed to have lived previous lives:

> At the same time they have often displayed
> behaviors or phobia that were either unusual in their
> family or not explained by any current life events.
> In many cases of this type the child's statements

have been shown to correspond accurately to facts
in the life and death of a deceased person; in many
of these cases the families concerned have had no
contact before the case developed.

My view is that while the reincarnation event is a real nonlocal
event experienced by the child, the interpretation of the event is
incorrect. I believe the experiencer is in a high state of resonance
with the QH of the deceased and is able to retrieve QH information
about the dead person from that resonance condition. As the child
ages, rational left-brain processing begins to dominate, and the child
is no longer able to resonate with the QH of the deceased unless
trained to maintain that state of altered consciousness.

I would attribute a similar effect to someone who experiences
an out-of-body experience (OBE). Again, this most likely represents
a high state of resonance with the remote location. The experiencer
is probably retrieving and processing the QH of the objects at the
remote location that was visited nonlocally. This would account for
the phenomenon of a residual haunting. Such a haunting may not
be the replaying of an event of historical significance, but rather an
event as seen through the eyes of someone who witnessed it back in
history. The experiencer is seeing the ghost's version like a historical
Go-Pro video.

All Matter Interconnects with All Other Matter

At this most elementary level all matter interconnects with all
other matter, and this interconnection transcends space and time.
Theoretically, it is the basis for the most fundamental aspect of
consciousness—an undifferentiated awareness and perception that
extends up the evolutionary chain of increasing complexity.

All organisms, from the simplest to the most complex,
interconnect at a fundamental level using information obtained by
nonlocal quantum coherence. Every living organism communicates
with its environment and every other living organism through
coherent quantum emissions via the mechanism of the QH.

Quantum Holography

Quantum emissions from any material entity carry information nonlocally about its history of events. This is an evolving record of everything that has happened to that entity. These quantum emissions are in the form of EM waves of many different wavelengths. The information associated with these emissions is contained in interference patterns comprised of both the amplitude and the phase relationships of the emitted waves.

Interference patterns can carry an incredible amount of information, including the entire space-time history of living organisms. Mounting evidence shows that every physical object, both living and nonliving, has its own resonant holographic memory. This holographic image is stored in the Zero Point Field (ZPF).

Information in the ZPF is stored nonlocally and picked up via its resonance. We can think of any organism's QH as its nonlocal information store in the ZPF, created from all the quantum emissions of every atom, molecule and cell in the organism. Every objective, or physical experience of the organism, along with every subjective experience, is stored in its personal hologram, and the organism is in constant resonance with it. Each of us has unique resonant frequencies—our unique QH—which act as a "fingerprint" to identify the nonlocal information stored in the ZPF.

The QH is a kind of three-dimensional movie evolving in time. It fully describes everything about the states of the object that created it. The event history of all matter is continually broadcast nonlocally and stored in the QH. The information stored in the QH is recoverable through the process of resonance—not only resonance with the individual organism that created it, but also with other organisms if they can tap or tune into it. This is what we call "being psychic."

ZPF Storage Mechanism

The storage mechanism for quantum holograms resides in the ZPF. This field is accessible all around us but found nonlocally. It lasts indefinitely and can store unlimited quantities of information. It is not only nature's information storage mechanism, but also nature's information transfer mechanism. This information is emitted and absorbed by all objects and exists in a four-dimensional space time reality. QH applies to the smallest subatomic particle right up to the largest structures in the cosmos and takes place at all temperatures— even down to absolute zero.

For living organisms, QH applies to intra- and inter-communications between cells, organs and organ systems, and organisms and the larger environment, as suggested by Lipton, Sheldrake and several others. The concept applies to all living organisms on Earth as well as to all biological entities that exist throughout the cosmos. Whether abiotic or biotic, the entire event history of all matter anywhere in the universe is continuously broadcast nonlocally by coherent quantum emissions. This history is reabsorbed by an entity when received and interacts with all other matter and the ZPF through the exchange of quantum information.

EM Energy Carrying Information into the ZPF

German theoretical physicist Max Planck stated that electromagnetic energy is emitted or absorbed only in discrete quanta and forms the basis for the description of black body radiation. This was ultimately extended and used to describe how all matter absorbs and reemits photons (quanta of energy) from and into the Zero Point Field (ZPF) pervading all matter and even the vacuum of space, according to Bernard Haisch.

Normally these emissions are random exchanges of energy between particles and the ZPF. However, the emissions from complex matter (living organisms) exhibit quantum coherence and carry information nonlocally. Recall that the quantum phenomenon of nonlocality implies instantaneous transmission of information across space and time, according to David Darling.

Meta-analysis

Meta-analysis by parapsychologists Dean Radin and Jessica Utts (1991) across a large spectrum of experiments produced compelling statistics that show the perception of nonlocal information exists and is real. Meta-analysis is a new tool that has become essential in many of the soft sciences such as ecology, psychology, sociology and medicine. In meta-analysis, statistical methods are used to analyze the outcomes of entire collections of experiments that address a set of related research hypotheses.

Using meta-analysis of numerous psychic experiments, psychologist Gertrude Schmiedler isolated the "sheep and goat effect" in human behavior many decades ago. Sheep is a label for "believers," and goat is a label for "non-believers." Participants in human telepathy experiments exhibited results statistically above or below chance results depending on their subjective bias toward the experiment. Answers that were 100 percent wrong were considered as statistically significant as 100 percent correct answers. Both betrayed the mindset or intention of the subject. Only chance results were considered inconclusive.

A series of experiments investigating intentionality were meta-analyzed by Dr. Marilyn Schlitz, who found that experimenter bias affected the outcome even in double blind experiments. Thus, we have now learned that bias, belief and intention clearly have an effect in the realm of mind and consciousness studies. Non-believers are less likely to see or experience ghosts and UFOs, if ever. I have witnessed investigations in the most haunted buildings that provided no paranormal evidence because a member of the vigil was a non-believer or had the mindset of "prove it to me." This may be why individuals like professional skeptic James Randi has not found sufficient evidence of psychic phenomena in a TV studio in which a hostile audience of non-believers was present.

Based on my own experience, when you see your first UFO or ghost, you are more likely to see more. Seeing the first one shatters the non-believer mindset.

Cells Communicate through QH

The mechanism of QH also is used by the fifty to one hundred trillion cells in the human body. QH answers the question of how cells cooperate and work together to make a whole human. While cells are actively cooperating, thousands of them are dying every second. Over the course of one week, your body will have billions of new cells, yet you remain *you* with the same memories, the same functionality and the same distinct features.

Every single cell contains the same genetic blueprint of DNA. That DNA, along with environmental influences, exerts major influences over the development and functioning of those cells. But cells are not only subordinate to DNA—they function and maintain homeostasis by communicating and cooperating simultaneously with many other cells of the body and by using the information they receive from the environment.

Much of this inter-cellular signaling is electrochemical, but biologists still struggle with some aspects of the mechanisms. It is hard to imagine how as many as one hundred trillion cells can remain harmonized by the slow process of electrochemical signaling— especially at times when survival of the entire organism is at stake, which would require rapid and coordinated responses.

Resonance with an Object's or Living Organism's QH

Resonance with QH works in a way similar to how strings work on a guitar. Take two identical guitars, tune the corresponding strings on each guitar to the same frequencies, and then place them on opposite sides of a small room. Pluck a string on one of the guitars and the corresponding string on the other guitar will begin to vibrate in resonance with the first guitar.

Vibrating strings on each guitar produces a standing wave. The vibrations cause the wave to travel down the string to the point at which the string is attached to the guitar. The wave then reflects off that point and travels in the opposite direction, like a mirror image of the original wave. As the original wave meets the reflected wave, they will interfere with each other and transmit a new standing wave through the air.

Add a third identically tuned guitar to the room. If the corresponding strings on two of the guitars are plucked simultaneously at the same place on the string, the corresponding string on the third guitar will begin to vibrate—but with one slight difference. Since both plucked strings were struck at the same string location at the same time, the sound waves produced from each will constructively interfere with and reinforce each other in the air resulting in sound waves of greater amplitude. The string on the third guitar resonates with *greater amplitude* (volume).

Repeat this process with a fourth guitar. The amplitude of the resonating standing wave will continue to increase. This strengthening of the resonating wave is important when accessing information stored in the ZPF. The larger the amplitude of the standing wave, the easier it is for another object to resonate with it.

The guitar analogy helps explain how information is stored in the QH with the ZPF. Since the brain operates as massively parallel quantum computers, it can set up a resonant condition with microtubules scattered throughout the brain, each tuned to the same frequency as the standing waves produced by the same frequency in the ZPF.

A Useful Model

We now have a mechanism to describe how mind can manipulate matter. The QH is a model of how reality works. Like all models, it enables us to make predictions and interpret how nature operates. It explains many effects, including aspects of mind, memory and stream of consciousness, and factors affecting health, psychic events, Jung's collective unconscious, the Akashic record, and other phenomena produced by the resonance with the QH that resides in the ZPF. Before the discovery of QH we had no mechanism to account for these phenomena, let alone for the implied transfer of information between objects.

This model explains how living organisms know and use non-native information. It elevates the fundamental status of information in nature to that of matter and energy. It offers an explanation for how the whole of creation learns, self-corrects and evolves as a self-organizing, interconnected, holistic system. Since the laws of nature appear to be consistent throughout the universe, there is no reason this model should not also apply to the consciousness of extraterrestrials or those in spirit.

The Biology of Transmitting and Receiving

How is information transmitted to and received by a Zero Point Field? Sir Roger Penrose is a mathematician, physicist, and professor at Oxford University; in conjunction with Stuart Hameroff, an anesthesiologist and professor at the University of Arizona, he proposed that microtubules in brain cells might be responsible for fundamental forms of perception. Microtubules provide the foundation for the emergence of higher orders of consciousness in species possessing a brain.

Microtubules are hollow cylindrical polymers of a protein called tubulin that organize cellular activities. These protein lattices exist in the cell's cytoskeleton, which is found within the brain's neurons. Penrose and Hameroff claimed that quantum mechanical effects within each tubulin govern tubulin states. These effects function as a quantum computer using quantum bits that interact nonlocally with other tubulins and with the QH. When enough tubulins entangle long enough to reach a specific threshold, a "conscious event" occurs. Each event results in a state that regulates classical neural activities, such as the triggering of neural firings, which ultimately affects perception, learning and memory.

Like one big collective, we share the same atoms and molecules. The vibration level of each atom allows information to pass from one atom to another according to quantum physics.

Penrose and Hameroff corroborated this theory in the 2011 April/May edition of the *Journal of Cosmology*. They suggested that the human brain resonates—that our brains act like quantum receivers and transmitters. The recent discovery of quantum vibrations in microtubules validated their previous work on tubulins. They also suggested that EEG rhythms (brainwaves) derive from vibrational computations, orchestrated by synaptic inputs and stored memories in microtubules. Clinical trials of brain stimulation aimed at microtubule resonances have shown reported improvements in mood and may prove useful against Alzheimer's disease and brain injuries in the future.

How we Recognize and Perceive

This resonance process is called Phase Conjugate Adaptive Resonance (PCAR). It is the basis for the most fundamental level of perception in all living organisms according to Edgar Mitchell. Bats, dolphins and whales use sonar to send out signals and then receive reflected signals to locate targets. PCAR is the brain analog of that process. QH operates similarly—emissions from bio-matter carry information about the entire organism. Stem cell research supports this concept.

The Brain Creates Real Experiences

The brain processes and stores information holographically as a massively parallel computer system. Karl H. Pribram and others have demonstrated this in the laboratory with animals and in operating theaters with humans. In the human studies, the brain was exposed and stimulated with low voltage electrical signals while the patient was conscious and able to describe the resulting experience. The subjects have recalled extremely detailed and vivid memories as if reliving the remembered experiences. With electrical neurological input, animals have also recalled memories of how to run a maze successfully.

Pribram's (and others) human and animal experiments suggest brains store information holographically as images. Scientist

Peter Marcer compared this holographic storing of information to a detailed three-dimensional movie and stated that it generates a stream of consciousness of what the mind experiences.

To accomplish holographic processing the brain acts as a transmitter by sending a "virtual" signal to the object perceived. This results in a mirror signal received by the brain from the object. The brain acts as an information receptor, utilizing resonances with a specific range of EM frequencies (wavelengths). The resulting resonance sets up a standing wave between the object and the brain. So an EMF reading is recordable moments before and during paranormal contact, as previously documented. So the thoughts of the ghosts are recorded rather than the entity itself—if the deceased is required to think itself into a location in order to haunt it.

Information in Energy

Information is nothing more than the data contained in patterns of matter or energy. The meaning derived from these patterns is interpreted in the mind of the percipient based on prior knowledge, memory and beliefs. The more knowledge and experience we gain, the more likely we will be able to interpret an event objectively and accurately.

Soaked into an Environment

When we visit a sacred place of worship, like an ancient chapel or medieval cathedral, it is hard not to feel a sense of awe and reverence. Over the centuries, countless people have entered these buildings with the same feelings, and these are absorbed into the structure of the buildings over time through the quantum emission of the people and resonance with the atoms and molecules of the structures. The longer people are exposed to the environment and resonance over time, the more coherence is achieved with these molecules and atoms. This coherence remanifests as emissions back into the environment, which then resonates with the visitors. The result can be a subjective feeling of awe and reverence—exactly what one would expect when entering a holy site. This is an example of PCAR as a group phenomenon, according to Schempp.

Other examples of this phenomenon include feelings of fright and horror experienced at sites considered to be haunted, such as battlefields or murder sites. In haunted house attractions, fear experienced by visitors can be pushed into the environment and reexperienced by subsequent visitors. The Soap Factory on the banks of the Mississippi River in Minneapolis is a nineteenth century warehouse once used for the process of soap production. It now hosts one of the most celebrated haunted house attractions in the Twin Cities. I believe the visitors passing through and experiencing fear and horror in turn imprint those emotions into the structure of the building.

I personally experienced this at the London Dungeon in South London, a themed tourist attraction depicting the history of torture and the macabre with realistic tableaus and live actors. The original site was developed in a location used purely for storage—no one had died there, and no trauma had taken place. Yet the site felt very tense and nervous with an overlay of apprehension and fear. I believe these emotions had been imprinted into the environment by the millions of annual visitors who had exhibited these very emotions.

We seem to live in a participatory universe. There is no such thing as pure objective reality—we influence everything that we interact with. Every object influences every other object. This is why we feel positive energy from some people while others seem to project negative energy. We can implant positive or negative energy into any living organism or inanimate object.

I experienced an inanimate object holding negative energy when I held the ax used in a mass murder in 1917. The incident had occurred near Clement in Minnesota. Without motive or provocation, a farmer attacked and killed his four children and wife with an ax and then hung himself at the site. The Redwood County Museum has the ax on display, and I had the opportunity to hold the gruesome murder weapon. It was a horrid, buzzy, angry object. I held it in both hands and felt many kinds of negative emotions coming from it. As simply a piece of wood with a forged metal head, it should not have projected such energy and feelings.

Objects Gaining a QH

Establishing resonance (PCAR) between a percipient and a target object creates a QH for that object. This is achieved by a mirrored relationship between our experience of the target object in terms of our thoughts and through our senses and the same reciprocal signals the target object is sending back. When the object is inanimate, like an apple, our interest is on the non-local information obtained by the percipient about the apple. But information about the percipient is also available to the apple. The resonant condition between the two is a reciprocal relationship.

How Nature Learns and QH Ghosts

The QH model predicts that the history of events for the target object—an apple, in the case above—is carried in the apple's QH. This implies that *attention* or *intention* is focused on the apple by the percipient and causes that specific event to be recorded in the apple's QH. Therefore, a residual haunting could be defined as the percipient giving attention or intention to an event he is witnessing, and then the event is recorded as a QH. If the event goes unwitnessed, then a residual haunting of it cannot exist. In another example, seeing the ghost of your grandmother in her bedroom may actually be your grandmother as seen by you or someone else in her bedroom when she was alive but is now being presented to you as a QH after she died.

We cannot question the apple or the residual haunting of your grandmother to ask them about their experiences. But the apple's interaction will create a phase shift in the apple's QH, which should be detectable. This phenomenon is rooted in natural and primitive nonlocal physical processes that are fundamental to the interaction between all objects, living or not.

This means that when witnessing a residual haunting, the experiencer may be seeing someone else's experience. When Harry Martindale saw the Roman army marching through the cellar of the Treasurer's House in York, England in 1953, he was seeing the experience of someone else who had witnessed that event in real time a thousand years ago while standing on the side of the road. If no one had witnessed the Roman soldiers, the residual haunting could not happen.

The information received after seeing or experiencing an event is processed by brain functions to provide cognition and assign meaning, such as "I am seeing and hearing a Roman army march along the road." Cognition and meaning require the brain to find a relationship between the perceived information and the information residing in the percipient's memory. This information is interpreted based on the beliefs and prior experience stored in the percipient's memory, such as "I have a previous experience and understanding of what a Roman army looks like, and I am aware of the action of marching." The viewer can then form intent with respect to the object. In such cases the output labeled *action* changes from *attention* (passive state) to *intention* (proactive state).

In self-aware animals, cognition, meaning and intent as related to an external object is described in simple terms—enemy, fight, flight, food, and greet. The nonlocal component of information, although present and creating effect, is operating below the level of conscious perception in humans and results in instinctual subconscious behaviors in animals.

The resonant condition (PCAR) implies a symmetry whereby information flows in both directions between the object and the percipient so that each is both target object and percipient to the other. This means that the Roman Army's own awareness of its marching is added to the witnessing of its marching.

Black Holes and Mysticism

Quantum physics suggests that black holes are nature's hard drive within the universe. They swallow and process information and quantum holograms. Information, then, is never lost. All of time past and present is stored and accessible as in a giant repository.

What is a Black Hole?

A black hole is a region of space formed from a dying star. Its internal pressures are so great that its neutrons cannot counterbalance its own gravity. In a black hole, matter compresses to such an infinitely small density that the normal laws of physics break down. Nature, electrons, protons, carbon elements, collapsing extremes of heat, light, temperature, density, gravity, and all of quantum mechanical behavior is mixed with gas clouds. The entire thing collapses without limit if enough gas is present. Nothing can escape a black hole's gravitational field—not even light.

This process of collapse creates negative energy in the universe called dark matter because it sits between stars and has no illumination. Dark matter is the glue that keeps the universe from spinning off in all directions. It holds solar systems together. The black hole in our galaxy is Sagittarius A. It has the equivalent mass of ten million of our suns. The farther away objects are from a black hole, the less gravitation pull is applied to them. The point at which an object cannot be sucked into the black hole or accelerate away is called the event horizon. At the event horizon an object outside the black hole is simply held in static position.

Black Holes Preserve Information

Tiny particles can avoid the gravitational pull of a black hole in the event horizon due to a phenomenon called *quantum teleportation*. The information is stored in the event horizon as static microwaves and disseminated into the universe as a qubit, creating a network for a consciousness, a higher guiding intelligence.

Microwaves are everywhere around us and carry information. Information is a pattern of energy—a light wave for example. Microwaves are a form of electromagnetic radiation. Before the advent of fiber optic transmission, most long-distance telephone calls were carried over networks of microwave radio relay links. Microwaves travel very fast. Only if it were possible to make these microwaves static, however, could the information stored within them be accessed. Local observers would see it move slower and slower and becoming more red.

This information is disseminated through qubits, tiny pieces of information that store data about a particle, such as the direction of its spin. In a mind-bending study, researchers at the California Institute of Technology demonstrated that a piece of qubit information could escape from a black hole. When a qubit falls into a black hole it may be able to mysteriously escape using quantum teleportation.

Scientists previously applied this phenomenon to teleport a qubit over a distance of eighty-nine miles. The qubit retrieval protocol can be understood using very basic quantum mechanics. However, a true understanding of the effects of a black hole would likely require physics well beyond conventional quantum mechanics and semi-classical black hole physics.

Hawking's Black Hole ZPF Theory

The celebrated physicist Professor Stephen Hawking suggested a similar theory in a 2016 scientific paper published in *Physical*

Review Letters. The paper described zero-energy particles known as *soft hair* that store information in the event horizon. These hairs could solve the central paradox of black holes by backing up the basic laws of the universe, which state that anything that has ever existed is preserved via its information.

Hawking's theory uses Magnetospheric Eternally Collapsing Objects (MECOs), black holes with electrically charged magnetic fields. MECOs are found in vast numbers around the universe and are the most powerful source of energy and power in our universe. MECOs have a high-density surface. Astronomer Dr. Rudolph E. Schild claims to have found evidence of such a magnetic field from the quasar Q0957+561. It is important to distinguish between a black hole and a MECO. MECOs are fundamentally the same as black holes, but with no event horizon and a strong magnetic field measured as billions and billions of gauss. In a MECO, magnetic fields try to push out the spinning magnetic flow as the flow is trying to come in because of the immense gravitational pull. X-rays create luminosity as positive ions and negative electrons come together creating a luminous spiral disc that tries to enter the black hole. This phenomenon is visible with the Hubble Telescope.

MECOs and black holes are a source of greater power. If you believe in a higher being, black holes and MECOs would reside inside that higher power. They are mechanisms by which the universe can manifest the will and intent of the creator but still allow for free will. Our freewill meets predicted possibilities—a way of being where we can decide our own outcomes and fate, but within a framework created by a higher being that can impose their own will or outcomes at any moment.

Black holes and MECOs can prove that ghosts and UFOs are real by explaining how they can exist. They also quantify a Devine Being—remember, on the first day God created the heavens and the stars.

Quantum Physics is Mystical

A holistic universe is a mystical system. Scientific theories claiming all things and people interconnect in a non-empirical realm of the world are mystical in nature. Swiss psychologist Aniela Jaffé described this in her book *Was C. G. Jung a Mystic? And Other Essays*:

> Both Junguian psychology and mysticism deal with the experience of the numinous. The difference is that mysticism speaks of an encounter with God and lets the matter test at that. Jungian psychology also speaks of an encounter with God, in the sense that "God" represents the word or the designation for something incognizable and incomprehensible. For both, God is a primordial human experience...

So quantum physics is actually a form of mysticism, and so is Jung's psychology.

The evolution of human thinking is characterized by the discovered truths regarding the order of the world, truths that are so fundamental they appear repeatedly in the minds of different people of different ages and in different parts of the world. The Indian sages called this phenomenon "Sanatana Dharma." In the sixteenth century, Italian humanist Agostino Steuco introduced the concept into Western philosophy as "perennial philosophy." I consider this phenomenon a special form of synchronicity. It shows that ours is a mystical mind because it is connected with a cosmic background that has mind-like properties.

Ancient concepts of the world constantly reemerge in our thinking, but in an evolving way. For example, Greek philosopher Plato claimed that true reality resides in a realm of ideas outside the visible world. This is similar to the claim that the empirical world actualizes out of a realm of virtual quantum forms. Nevertheless, the quantum view isn't identical with the Platonic view. Rather, it is mathematical, quantitative, and has led to countless practical applications that have changed our way of life. In the same way, Jung's descriptions of the human psyche may be similar to ancient views but are evolved versions of them. We believe that the evolution of concepts and our understanding of them is the true function of biological evolution. It is impossible to know whether we are evolving with the cosmic mind or whether it is our mind that has to evolve to better understand a non-evolving cosmic order.

The practice of mysticism is an example of an evolving process. I don't mean it is identical with ancient religious practices, but it shares essential aspects with ancient practices in an evolved way. In the book *Was C. G. Jung a Mystic?* Jaffé describes aspects of Jung's mysticism that confirm this view:

> If the concept "mystic" suggests the immediate experience of the numinous or the perceiving of an originally hidden transcendent reality, the "other side," then it involves an experience which also plays a central role in Jung's approach to analytical psychology; that is, the consideration of images and contents which enter into consciousness from the hidden background of the psyche, the collective unconscious. (...) [which] must be conceived of as a realm with neither space nor time that eludes any objective knowledge. What we perceive are its effects.

William James' thesis "The Varieties of Religious Experiences: A Study in Human Nature" shows that twenty-first century science can no longer deny the non-empirical:

> [The] unseen region in question is not merely ideal, for it produces effects in this world. When we commune with it, work is actually done upon our finite personality, for we are turned into new men, and consequences in the way of conduct follow in

the natural world upon our regenerative charge. But
that which produces effects within another reality
must be termed a reality itself, so I feel as if we had
no philosophical excuse for calling the unseen or
mystical world unreal.

The main goal of every spiritual tradition is to unite with the
transcendent reality. Different traditions may give different names
to the Divine, but in all of them we find the same desire to become
one with the Divine. Psychically, that state can adopt the symbolic
and transformational meaning of rebirthing, synonymous with
becoming one with the Self. Jung states this in his book *Psychology
and Religion: West and East. Volume 11*:

> To the Indian it is clear that the self as the originating
> ground of the psyche is not different from God, and
> that, so far as a man is in the self, he is not only
> contained in God but actually is God. Shri Ramana
> is quite explicit on this point. The goal of Eastern
> religious practice is the same as that of Western
> mysticism: the shifting of the center of gravity
> from the ego to the self, from man to God. This
> means that the ego disappears in the self, and man
> in God.

Spiritual Dark Matter and the Paranormal

Rudy Schild suggested that MECOs—this powerful source of
quantum information—are the machinery in which prayer can
reside. This machinery could then be accessed by another greater
intelligence. This concept could provide answers to why miracles
occur. If you believe God exists, miracles and answered prayers may
come out of this process.

Relationship to the Paranormal

How are quantum holograms and the storage of the universe's thoughts since the dawn of time applied to the paranormal field? Parapsychologist Dean Radin described a series of experiments conducted in the latter half of the twentieth century on a wide range of psychic phenomena. The results suggested that experimenters are obtaining far more correlations than can be expected by chance, achieved by performing experiments using a random number generator (RNG) and subjects attempting to predict and influence the numbers generated using psycho-kinesis (PK). This resulted with the odds against chance of thirty-five trillion to one over the entire database.

Radin's analysis followed a decade-long series of experiments by Robert G. Jahn at Princeton University. The experiments provided overwhelming evidence that human subjects could produce statistically skewed results in mechanical processes normally considered driven by random processes. A similar study with perceptual deprivation by Radin demonstrated results with odds of one in 29,000,000,000,000,000,000,000 against.

Radin has also discovered that audiences watching stage performances would skew the output of random number generators during periods of high emotional content in the performance. In a wide-ranging audience participation experiment, he recorded the output of computer random number generators during the television broadcasts of the O.J. Simpson murder trial. Most television news programs covered this event live for weeks with millions of viewers. The results of random number generators set up to monitor this event were skewed by the emotional peaks that occurred during the trial and by the number of people watching. A similar effect happened on September 11, 2001 at the time of the World Trade Center disaster in New York City.

This suggests we are more likely to see or use psychic skills during moments of high stress and anxiety. Therefore, exploring a house believed to be haunted, visiting the site of a murder or massacre, mourning the death of a loved one, or during the process of being abducted by aliens or upon seeing a UFO, one would be more likely to have a psychic experience. It helps, then, to be in the right place at the right time with the right set of emotions to see and hear paranormal phenomena.

The Princeton experiments report that intentionality of study participants created nonrandom effects to bias the skewed distribution. In the Radin experiments, the results were not the result of intentionality because the participants were unaware of the experiment. His hypothesis was that rapt attention drove the system away from randomness and toward greater order. Results suggest that attention and intention provide closely correlated outcomes. Being actively part of the process and believing it can happen influence results.

Many types of mind-to-mind or mind-to-object experiments have been rigorously and routinely conducted for decades with statistical significance. They are often dismissed or ignored by mainstream science, however, because the implications of nonlocal action are so foreign to the mainstream view of objectivism and the possibility of mind-matter interactions.

If resonance is necessary, specifically PCAR as described earlier, then we must also consider the perceived object or target and the percipient's perceptual system as traveling in a phase-locked resonant feedback loop. The incoming wave from the target carrying the emitted information may be labeled as "perception" from the viewpoint of the percipient, and the return path may be labeled as "attention" (or intention) depending on what the percipient is trying to achieve. Note, however, that this is a two-way street. The act of perceiving also affects the target object perceived! Therefore, we *do* live in a participatory universe.

There is no such thing as pure objectivity. In the case of nonlocal effects at a distance outside the body, simple correlation of entangled particles is the most basic form of perception. The correlations between entangled particles are reciprocal. Action on one particle creates an effect on other entangled particle instantaneously and across large distances. This phenomenon is no less important for macro scale objects.

Remote Viewing

I have already discussed the difference between *thinking you want to be somewhere and arriving* and the phenomenon of remote viewing (RV). But the theory of QH can explain how the phenomenon of RV works. RV allows us to describe and experience activities and events that the normal five senses cannot detect. Those participating in RV experiments are often provided with clues to the location of a target object such as a description or picture, location by latitude and longitude, or an icon representing the target. These clues are usually sufficient for the percipient to establish a resonance with the target. The receiver links perceptions with their own internal database of experiences in order to recognize and describe the target's attributes and obtain the perceived internal information.

When remotely viewing complex objects, the perceived information is seldom so unambiguous as to be instantly recognizable as correct. Sketches, metaphors and analogies are used to recognize and communicate the nonlocal information. A considerable amount of training, teamwork, and experience is necessary to reliably and correctly extract complex nonlocal information from a distant location. Skilled individuals frequently report the internal information as vivid, clear and unambiguous. The remote viewing information received in such cases is strictly non-local and based on the hypothesis of QH. The received information is missing the normal space-time component information from any of the five normal senses about the object, which is necessary to completely identify and specify it via resonance.

In most individuals, this intuitive mode of perception is enhanced by training. With practice, percipients can perceive greater detail, accuracy, and achieve greater reliability. Training can also cause the associated neural circuitry to become more robust. The use and practice of meditation in my own practice has facilitated better RV results. Reducing of stress, eliminating distractions, and quieting the mind through meditation has improved my own ability to focus, thereby improving the resonance condition.

Meditation

Those most practiced in meditation experience an altered sense of space-time, the dissolution of self, gain access to universal knowledge and sometimes feel a unified sense of oneness with all of existence. Along with this sense of oneness comes a feeling of bliss and a clarity of mind. Such meditators have entered into a state of high resonance with the QH and have access to all the information implied by such unification. This seems to describe the epiphany Edgar Mitchell experienced on his return flight from the moon.

In humans, it is a well-established meditation principle that prolonged, focused attention on an object causes the percipient and the target object to appear to merge so that a much deeper level of understanding about the object is obtained. This understanding would not have been available through classical space-time information. If I am ever asked by a client or student to name one thing they can do to make themselves psychic or develop their skills, I would say, "Meditate." I was not able to turn my psychic skills on and off until I learned to meditate. I cannot fully explain why meditation improves skills and increases psychic ability. But I know it works, so I will keep doing it. This is no different than a pregnant woman craving certain foods but not necessarily knowing why, though there is a reason.

The ability to quiet the mind is another benefit of meditation. As a Buddhist practitioner would say, "Quieting the mind is getting the monkey to sit on one branch instead of jumping around." If my mind is clear of all thought, it is easier to distinguish my thoughts and ideas from information being placed there by a third party such as a spirit or quantum information.

Being psychic is like daydreaming. When I am in a psychic mode, I am lucid and interacting with my client, but part of my mind is daydreaming. Meditation facilitates that process.

The mind and brain, with its one hundred billion neurons, function together as a massive information processor and can perform many tasks simultaneously. Most of this processing is subconscious, or in the right hemisphere, which is the seat of the intuitive part of the mind.

Conscious, focused attention takes place mostly in the left hemisphere in the cognitive part of the brain. Attention deficit disorder (ADD) is a disorder in which a percipient is unable to maintain a singular focus for a sufficient time to complete a desired task or observation, a necessary condition for resonance (PCAR) to be established with the perceived object. Particularly in the western tradition, academic interest has been primarily on left brain or rational processing rather than right brain intuitive functions. It is the left brain cognitive ability in humans that allows intuitive, creative and artistic processes to take place in the right brain. Given the fact that with training and practice all individuals can reestablish and deepen their cognitive access to intuitive, non-local information demonstrates that learning recall is taking place within the whole brain itself, and this learning involves enhanced coherence and coordination between the hemispheres and the QH.

I have organized and run many psychic development classes over the last ten years. I believe I can take any individual and train them to be psychic. In 2010, I worked with a student in Minnesota who did not believe she had any psychic skills. She now makes a good living from conducting psychic readings at healing and wellness expos all over the Midwest.

Healing

Healers know how important it is to focus, which creates a resonance with the object of their healing activities. Once in resonance, healers often report a picture appearing in their mind that displays as a three-dimensional holograph. Diseased or damaged tissues in the target often appear fuzzy or at least somehow different from the normal tissue surrounding them. Sometimes healers say they sense energy blockages. They claim an ability to focus energy or somehow manipulate with intentionality the diseased tissue that over time changes the appearance of the visualized image; the diseased tissue begins to take on the characteristics of the healthy tissue surrounding it, they say. Could this be the result of the intentionality of the healer resonating with the quantum emissions and subsequent absorptions by the diseased tissues?

A Reiki healer will place the healing energy of the universe into a client. It is irrelevant where the Reiki puts the energy so long as it enters the body. The body knows where the healing must go. I can spend a full session with my hands on the client's head, and if their issue is with their foot the healing will still go where needed.

George De La Warr was a British engineer who conducted experiments in the 1940s and 1950s on mechanisms associated with remote diagnosis and healing. De La Warr began experiments with his wife, an accomplished psychic healer, to detect the radiation emitted in such processes. At first, he thought this mechanism was related to some form of EM radiation, but later he realized it was associated with resonance. He eventually built a diagnostic device that acted as a resonant cavity. Perhaps the strangest aspect of the discovery was his wife's ability to produce a resonant condition between the target and the measuring device. She was also able to project this resonance condition onto a blank photographic plate. She was eventually able to pick up resonances from plants, trees, humans and even diseased tissues.

The De La Warrs compiled a library of several hundred photographic plates. In 2008, the photographs were analyzed by modern 3D CAD/CAM software that showed the images were spatially encoded with a 3D effect like those produced by fMRI machines but with higher resolution. These experiments, along with recent discoveries associated with fMRI machines, provide evidence that macro-scale quantum holography is a real phenomenon produced by conscious attention and intention of a percipient on objects of interest for healing.

Healing through Icons

Healers and people praying sometimes use icons in their endeavors, focusing their intentionality to resonate with the person targeted. Icons can be an image, picture, representation or even an article associated with the target of the intention. Icons of many types provide a mechanism for the healer to "tune in" or resonate with the target. Touching an icon seems to satisfy the resonant (PCAR) requirement and probably allows the intender access to information about the target that would be unavailable from normal space-time information. Police agencies often use this modality with psychics, who then focus their attention to gain information about a crime scene, often with considerable success.

QH theory suggests that useful icons have been in the presence of, or contain the signature information of, the person targeted for healing, so that the event history of the icon and that of the individual intersect. In the paranormal world the ability to gain unknown knowledge about places and individuals through touching or holding an object, such as a wedding ring, is called Psychometry. The phase relationships of the quantum emissions of the icon contain a record of the target object's journey in three-dimensional space and time, as well as the quantum states through which it has passed on this journey.

Reiki healers and other psychically sensitive individuals often enter into resonance with an icon or other object—Reiki symbols or a crucifix, for example—to focus their attention and intention. The Bible documents Jesus writing on the ground to provide a target to focus on:

John 8:6-8

They were using this question as a trap, in order to have a basis for accusing him.

But Jesus bent down and started to write on the ground with his finger. When they kept on questioning him, he straightened up and said to them, "Let any one of you who is without sin be the first to throw a stone at her." Again he stooped down and wrote on the ground.

Prayer

People praying for others may initiate a nonlocal resonance process—a collective positive intention—with a target object. Healing prayer has existed in all cultures for millennia. If prayer did not produce some positive results, it is likely religion would have abandoned it centuries ago. Healing prayer is attributed to supernatural forces rather than resonance with the target's QH. This is simply another example of phenomenology waiting for science to catch up.

A physician, Dr. Larry Dossey, and many others have attempted to document the efficacy of prayer, particularly healing prayer. Some claim the results establish the case for healing prayer. The difficulties of controlling all the clinical study variables like the experimenter effect, however, leave openings for valid criticism. Parapsychologist Dr. Dean Radin's studies show that attention alone produced nonlocal results in random event generators (REGs) and other machines.

Ghosts and UFOs are Information

Ghosts are quantum holograms. When a person dies, his or her quantum information is diffused but not forgotten. It is at a lower amplitude, so it looks fuzzy and semi-translucent. Sensitive people can see this. Einstein described energy transfer as previously discussed, but information can also transfer as energy in microwaves, and microwaves can travel through solids.

A UFO may be sent to a destination by operators inside the UFO or by the UFO itself—if it is a semi-sentient vehicle—via instantaneous thoughts (telepathy). Information, then, propagates in the universe faster than the speed of light. Einstein's proposition is correct for particles but not for information. The UFO is a self-scanning quantum hologram that projects itself to Earth like a ghost as follows:

1. Something is starting to happen—a "fuss."
2. Details emerge, a flat, translucent, onochromatic color.
3. It becomes totally colored and solid—looking completely "there."
4. Mass arrives.

In the first stage, the atmosphere changes, and equipment can start to register the mostly invisible ghost's arrival with EM readings and the blocking of wavelength signals. Shorted electrical circuits and mechanical malfunction are common.

In the second stage, A UFO begins to take shape. It starts to develop color and show detail.

In the third stage, a UFO has fully materialized and looks like a solid vehicle but is still lacking mass.

In the final stage, mass arrives, and the vehicle has obtained weight. A UFO can stop anywhere between these stages. Between stages three and four it activates an antigravity device or propulsion system to stop it from falling out of the sky. The difference between stage three and four also delineates between whether a rock can pass through the vehicle if thrown by a witness.

Applied to Ghosts

We can apply similar descriptive stages to the appearance of a ghost.

1. A pale, smoky, ethereal manifestation—something is starting to happen.
2. Details emerge; a flat, translucent, monochrome or faded color.
3. Fully manifested ghost with full color and detail.
4. Mass arrives.

I can provide detail for these stages from my own personal experiences and evidence. In stage 1, a smoky, ethereal anomaly commonly appears. I personally witnessed this in the bar area of the Palmer House Hotel, Minnesota.

The second stage presents the diaphanous, stereotypical ghost. I have added the elements of fading and appearing flat and monochromatic. One of our more experienced investigators saw a full-bodied apparition appear in the lobby of the Mound Theater in Minnesota when organizing an equipment case. He walked from the lobby to the dressing room and looked up to see a middle-aged man watching him through the open doors of the ticket booth. The ghost's eyes followed him, and they exchanged a glance. The man wore clothes from the 1950s with a period brown tweed suit, yellow tie, and black, sweptback hair. The investigator described the entity as faded in color like an old photograph. The apparition also appeared completely two-dimensional like a cardboard cutout. The ghost then disappeared.

In the third stage a ghost appears solid and can be mistaken for a living person. I suspect many of us have seen ghosts but failed to realize it. Ghosts can travel through walls and solid objects in this stage. They are still ethereal, however, despite a solid physical appearance. I believe a ghost can switch between this state and the final stage.

In the fourth stage, the ghost exhibits physical activity. It can throw objects, manipulate light switches, open doors, punch, claw and make the sound of footsteps.

Collective Consciousness Conclusion

Through psychology, ancient mystic teachings and contemporary theory in quantum and particle physics, I can provide a catchall hypothesis for the phenomena I have documented in this book. I believe the cornerstones of this hypothesis are built upon known and verified properties and processes of nature. Perhaps some are yet to be discovered. But everything I have proposed is testable.

All animals with brain wave activity can haunt. Because plants don't have respiration and no heartbeat, they cannot haunt.

Plants, however, have awareness of themselves, measurable energy, electrical activity, and a repository system for conscious activity.

Society has great difficulty accepting that thoughts, specifically intentionality, can cause action at a distance even though these phenomena have been the subject of much scientific scrutiny for centuries. Einstein described this phenomenon as "spooky action at a distance."

If a particle decays to produce two other particles, one takes the role of spin-up and the other the role of spin-down. They appear to know when they are measured and make an agreement between themselves despite distance and with no information transfer. They seem to know when they are being measured and still produce this result even if measured separately by two different individuals at the same time. This is quantum entanglement.

Quantum physics brings us a new kind of reality in which it is our task to unlock our potential and free us from our ignorance. In agreement with Jung's analytical psychology, quantum physics provides us with suggestions of how we can live in accordance with the numinous realm of the universe. That universe is so infinitely and finely structured and tuned for us to exist in that forces other than luck and randomness must exist.

Quantum physics not only proves ghosts and UFOs, but also the existence of a higher being—God.

Conclusion

This book presents a hypothesis based on my attempt to understand my personal experiences and those of many others. It strives to provide the "how" and "why" of those experiences when other explanations are in short supply or fall short of academic scrutiny. It is an attempt to make sense of the whole when only a small number of pieces are available. In trying to deliver on that goal, this book has been the most complicated and exhausting writing project I have ever undertaken.

I first committed my thoughts to paper over eight years ago. Then my ideas and concepts began to evolve as I witnessed paranormal phenomena during my investigations. Through my interactions with ufologists, personal UFO encounters and study, I realized my thoughts and ideas also applied to UFOs and the way aliens operate.

Besides my passion for ghosts and history, I also have a great interest in UFOs. But wading through the thousands of declassified UFO documents, when most were nothing more than spurious sightings by dubious witnesses over half a century ago, was very hard work. Reading page after page of abduction reports and hypnotherapy documents left me battle weary, and the eight years between the germination of this book to its fruition was a labor of love. Yet, within the deluge of historical documentation and reports, occasionally a diamond would appear—a glimmer of information that would stand out as evidence to corroborate and prove hypotheses.

These pivotal moments began to build into a body of work that has finally come together.

I needed to be many things in this book—a paranormal investigator, historian, ufologist, researcher, physicist, psychologist, theologian, astronomer and philosopher. The need to present the multitude of research and facts in an accessible manner tested my authorship skills to the fullest extent. The many disciplines I studied took me to very taxing and involved places. I have avoided physics all my life—much to the consternation of my physics teacher decades ago. My father worked in the physics laboratories of the Queen Mary and Westfield College in London, and I am sure I have been a constant disappointment to him with my creative, psychic, and metaphysical ways, so with every quantum physics book I opened I heard my father chuckling to himself in my head.

I studied psychology as a history methodology as part of my art history qualifications. If you know what happens to artists in their lifetimes, you can understand why they painted the way they did. The study of the life of Dutch painter Vincent Van Gogh would be the prime example. I lived with a psychologist for many years and gained knowledge through osmosis. Philosophy also played a large part in my art history studies.

It is common practice for an author to write the conclusion first. This gives the author an understanding of his ultimate goal. I wrote this conclusion over eight years ago as academic convention. I confess now, however, that I completely discarded my conclusion when the book was finished, which highlights how dramatically the text evolved. I never could have imagined the journey I have taken from interviewing abductees, witnessing ghosts and UFOs, and studying quantum theory, to studying the release of newly declassified documents on a weekly basis. Even now, after typing this sentence, contemporary science has discovered more about the universe, and the government has released many more documents.

UFOs and ghosts share many incredible and remarkable similarities. UFOs are the vehicles that aliens use as their mode of transport to traverse the great distances across the universe. Ghosts are the visible spirits of the deceased. These two phenomena could not be more polemically different from one another on the surface. Yet in your hands is a book dedicated to their similarities, a whole wedge of information set down in the middle of a UFO-and-ghost Venn diagram, much of it previously unconsidered.

I started this project fully believing in UFOs. As documented in this book, I have witnessed many credible sightings, and statistically it is probable that life exists in many parts of the universe. I have spent most of my adult life investigating ghosts, hauntings and paranormal activity. I have interacted with ghosts on a level that has spawned many history books based on the information and knowledge communicated to me—information that was previously lost to society.

I must admit to my initial skepticism at the information presented by some individuals who claimed abduction and in most cases abuse. But after the many years I dedicated to researching those aspects, I now believe. When I first researched abduction stories, I felt the ones that seemed more fanciful should be edited out. I am a skeptic when it comes to a high percentage of UFO and ghost sightings. I will try everything possible to ferret out false evidence or find an alternative explanation besides the paranormal. But there were many incidents and cases that defied logical explanation and sit firmly outside of normality. I realized when dealing with unimaginable concepts, like beings from other worlds and modes of travel outside of current human thinking, that any reports or documentation of an abduction should be reasonable and subject to exacting scrutiny based on what we do and don't know.

I have gained a valuable insight into my own practice as a psychic and paranormal investigator by looking at the canon of ufology. I always wondered why I appeared to attract more ghostly activity and UFO sightings than other paranormal investigators and ufologists. I would see paranormal teams leaving historic haunted buildings disappointed by their lack of activity on vigils. I questioned why this would occur when my own investigations in those same locations were so productive.

I also considered why I seemed to be a catalyst for more UFO sightings than most. I initially believed that a more visually aware person such as myself, with a background in the visual arts, may see more of what presents itself around them. Putting myself into situations where I am more likely to receive contact also facilitates a greater chance of experiencing such things. The more you look at the sky, the greater your chance of witnessing a UFO. I conducted twenty-eight paranormal investigations last year in some of the most haunted buildings across the Midwest. By default, then, I have a greater chance of having a paranormal experience. I have never been to a baseball game, but I know they exist. If I visited a stadium I would more than likely see a baseball game.

I now increasingly believe that my training and qualification as a Reiki Master may have a bearing on the frequency of my sightings and interactions. To be able to generate energy would certainly be a beacon for any UFO or passing ghost, and I have discussed in this book the way EMF connects both phenomena.

In many ways, the title of this book is misleading. Perhaps it should reflect the differences and things they do NOT have in common, not the similarities. I believe it would have been a shorter text. Obviously, ghosts and UFOs are not the same. One is the manifestation of a spirit that was once a physical person now deceased. The other is a non-terrestrial being most probably from outside our own galaxy that uses a vehicle to transcend the vastness of space. But there is certainly enough evidence to suggest they employ similar ways of being and traveling.

Ghosts and UFOs are both soaked in the lore and history of humankind through stories, pictures, documents and entertainment. Both can elicit fear and terror in the human psyche, both can cause stress and concern. Both can display the qualities of being solid and physical as well as the ability to appear and disappear at will through the power of thought—or through the use of a conceptual mechanism like a portal. Both have shown a history of relaying messages to man. Both are still unproven because of the limitations of contemporary science. Both provide a catalyst for man's need to explore and discover more about their nature by using the same equipment and data collection. Both can generate energy and olfactory experiences.

The dead may not fully understand how they can skip from the physical to the nonphysical. This is no different than the way I use my car and cell phone—with very little understanding of how either functions and operates. Yet I still journey and communicate using those devices. Because extraterrestrials have clearly mastered their devices, you would have to assume they have a full understanding of what they are doing and why.

Who knows how life has evolved in distant galaxies. We must stop trying to press our own limitations and shortcomings onto beings we have no knowledge of. Just because we can't think ourselves to another destination does not mean that others outside our own understanding cannot do this. This is true of the concepts provided by quantum theory when applied to paranormal means.

During my research, I was surprised by the way in which quantum theory describes the world and has taken science into the center of ancient spiritual teachings. For example, molecular wave functions have no units of matter or energy—they are pure, non-material forms. The same is true for Jung's archetypes. Like the wave functions of quantum systems, they are pure, non-material forms. In Aristotle's metaphysics, all things are mixtures of matter and form. There was only one pure form—God.

The term "virtual states" that quantum physicists apply to the empty states of atoms and molecules seems like a strange expression, yet Meister Eckhart, a medieval Dominican Monk and Mystic, invented the concept:

> The visible things are out of the oneness of the
> divine light.

Eckhart also wrote that their existence in the empirical world is due to the "Actualization of their 'virtual being.'"

The same unusual term appears in the mind of a medieval mystic, and then hundreds of years later in the mind of quantum physicists. This example shows that absolute truths can appear over and over with the same messages through thousands of years—in different minds, different ages and in different parts of the world. It is difficult to avoid the impression that our minds all connect to a cosmic realm of thoughts—the realm of Jung's archetypes. I certainly could not have imagined when I first wrote the conclusion for this book eight years ago that my study into the similarities between ghosts and UFOs would end in a place where I used scientific theory to prove a collective consciousness and that God can exist.

So much of what I have discussed happens in another part of the universe or in a different dimension yet affects us directly on Earth in the here and now. The way I and others have experienced changes in surroundings and atmosphere during and before a paranormal encounter is an example. It is almost like we have a moment of removal away from the framework of normality without even knowing that we are leaving the path. Even the most skeptical person is detoured—it is not the sole preserve of the believer. And in this small detour from the line of normality, others cannot see what the experiencer sees... they cannot engage with or even recognize what is very real to that individual at that moment. Even time seems to behave in odd ways. Then, as quickly as they leave the path, they are back inside the framework of normality once again with the same recognizable world around them, and all the laws of physics and time as we know it fit back into place. The experiencer, though, may never know that they left the path for that shortest of time. This sounds a lot like dissociative identity disorder (DID) or multiple personality disorder (MPD). But the experiencer receives physicality on that journey—radiation burns from UFO contact or recordings of the spirit talking to the experiencer.

I am now waiting for science to catch up and prove the things I have discussed in this book. I will prophesy that in the near future an example of life will be found on the planet Mars. This small microbe will allow man to believe that life is possible in almost all places across the universe. The first unequivocal contact between man and extraterrestrials will also take place when the general public will arrive first at a Roswell-type incident and capture cell phone video of the wreckage and alien bodies. The video will be instantly uploaded and shared to millions around the globe on social media before the government and military can arrive to remove the evidence and claim ignorance.

This book sits firmly in this era, and only history will be the judge of the ideas I have presented.

Bibliography

Baruss, I. *Science as a Spiritual Practice*. Imprint Academic; Exeter, UK, 2007.

Bullard, Thomas E. *The Myth and Mystery of UFOs*. University Press of Kansas, 2010.

Campbell, J. *The Hero with a Thousand Faces*. New World Library; Novato, California, USA, 2008. First published in 1949.

Condon, E.U., Project Director, and D. S. Gillmor, Editor. *Scientific Study of Unidentified Flying Objects*. Bantam Books, New York, 1968.

Curwen, Eliot Cecil. *Sussex Notes and Queries*. 1937. p. 139-140.

Eddington, A.S. *The Philosophy of Physical Science*. Macmillan; New York, NY, USA, 1939.

Eddington, A.S. *The Nature of the Physical World*. Macmillan; New York, NY, USA, 1929.

Forman, R.K.C., editor. *The Innate Capacity: Mysticism, Psychology, and Philosophy*. Oxford University Press; Oxford, UK, 1998.

Forman, R.K.C. *Mystical Consciousness, the Innate Capacity, and the Perennial Psychology*. Oxford University Press; Oxford, UK, 1999.

Green, Elmer & Alyse. *Beyond Biofeedback*. Knoll Publishing Company INC., 1977.

Haftmann, W. *Painting in the Twentieth Century*. Praeger; New York, NY, USA, 1965.

Hawking, Stephen. *A Brief History of Time: From the Big Bang to Black Holes*. Bantam Books, 1988.

Henderson, J.L. *Ancient Myths and Modern Man*. Jung C.G., editor. *Man and His Symbols*. Dell Publishing Co. Inc.; New York, NY, USA, 1964.

Jaffé, A. *Was C. G. Jung a Mystic? And Other Essays*. Daimon Verlag; Einsiedeln, Switzerland, 1989.

James, W. *The Varieties of Religious Experiences: A Study in Human Nature*. Longmans Green & Co.; London, UK, 1904.

Jung, C.G. *Flying Saucers: A Modern Myth of Things in the Sky*. MFL Books, New York, 1978.

Jung, C.G. *Psychology and Religion: West and East*. Volume 11 Princeton University Press; Princeton, NJ, USA, 1958. Collected Works.

Jung, C.G. *Mysterium Coniunctionis*. Volume 14 Princeton University Press; Princeton, NJ, USA, 1970. Collected Works.

Jung, C.G. *Psychology and Alchemy*. Volume 12 Princeton University Press; Princeton, NJ, USA. 1968. Collected Works.

Jung, C.G. *The Red Book: Liber Novus*. Shamdasani S., editor. Norton & Co.; New York, NY, USA, 2009.

Jung, C.G. *The Structure and Dynamics of the Psyche*. Volume 8. Princeton University Press; Princeton, NJ, USA, 1960. Collected Works.

Jung, C.G. *The Archetypes and the Collective Unconscious*. Volume 9. Princeton University Press; Princeton, NJ, USA, 1969. Collected Works.

Kafatos, M., Nadeau, R. *The Conscious Universe*. Springer; New York, NY, USA, 1990.

Klass, Philip J. *UFOs: The Public Deceived*. Prometheus Books, 1983.

Lang, Craig R. *The Cosmic Bridge: Close Encounters and Human Destiny*. Lulu Enterprises INC., 2006-2007.

Lang, Craig R. & McNeff, William. *An Extraterrestrial Odyssey*. Lulu Enterprises INC., 2013.

Mack, John E. *Abduction: Human Encounters with Aliens*. Macmillan Publishing Company, 1994.

Margry, Peter Jan. *Reframing Dutch Culture: Between Otherness and Authenticity. Progress in European Ethnology* (illustrated ed.). Ashgate Publishing, 2007. pp. 150–1. ISBN 9780754647058.

Molineux, Will. *Sciotericum Telescopicum: or a new Contrivance of adapting a Telescope to a Horizontal Dial, for Observing the Moment of Time by Day or* Night (1686). Kessinger Publishing, LLC, 2010.

Monod, J. *Chance and Necessity*. Collins; London, UK, 1972.

Newton, I. *Opticks*. 2nd ed. Dover Publications; New York, NY, USA, 1979. First published in 1704.

Plott, Robert. *The Natural History of Stafford-shire (1686)*. EEBO Editions, ProQuest, 2011.

Randle, Kevin. *Project Blue Book Exposed*. Marlowe & Company, New York, 1997.

Rife, Philip L. *It Didn't Start with Roswell: 50 Years of Amazing UFO Crashes, Close Encounters and Cover-ups*. Writers Club Press, 2001.

Russell, B. *History of Western Philosophy*. London University; London, UK, 1979. First published in 1946.

Schäfer, L. *In Search of Divine Reality*. University of Arkansas Press; Fayetteville, AR, USA, 1997.

Schäfer, L. *Em Busca de la Realidad Divina*. Lumen Publishing; Buenos Aires, Argentina, 2007.

Schäfer, L. *Versteckte Wirklichkeit—Wie uns die Quantenphysik zur Transzendenz führt (Hidden Reality: How Quantum Physics Will Lead Us to Transcendence)*. Hirzel; Stuttgart, Germany, 2004.

Schäfer, L. *Electron Diffraction as a Tool of Structural Chemistry*. J. Appl. Spectros, 1976.

Schäfer, L. *The gradient revolution in structural chemistry: The significance of local molecular geometries and the efficacy of joint quantum mechanical and experimental techniques*. J. Mol. Struct., 1983.

Schäfer, L. *Nonempirical reality: Transcending the physical and spiritual in the order of the One.* Zygon, 2008.

Schäfer, L. *Quantum reality, the emergence of complex order from virtual states, and the importance of consciousness in the universe.* Zygon, 2006.

Schäfer, L. *Quantum Reality and Evolution Theory.* J. Cosmol, 2009.

Schäfer, L. *A Response to Carl Helrich: The Limitations and Promise of Quantum Theory.* Zygon, 2006.

Schäfer, L. *A Response to Erwin Laszlo: Quantum and Consciousness.* Zygon, 2006.

Schäfer, L. *A Response to Stanley Klein: A Dialogue on the Relevance of Quantum Theory to Religion.* Zygon, 2006.

Schäfer, L., Diogo, D.P., Roy S. *Quantum Reality and Ethos: A Thought Experiment Regarding the Foundation of Ethics in Cosmic Order.* Zygon, 2009.

Schäfer, L. *Infinite Potential: What Quantum Physics Reveals about How We Should Live.* Random House Inc.; New York, NY, USA, 2013.

Thayer, G.D. *Radio Reflectivity of Tropospheric Layers.* Vol. 5, No. 11, 1970. pp. 1293-1299.

Von Franz, M.L. *Psyche and Matter.* Shamballa Pub.; Boston, MA, USA, 1992.

Wait, J.R. *Electromagnetic Waves in Stratified Media.* Pergamon Press, Oxford. Penguin Classics; Rev. Ed. Edition, 1962. pp 85-95.

Websites

Accessed between 2010-2019

https://www.express.co.uk/news/weird/783479/TR-3B-UFO-Cooper-Nuclear-Station-Nebraska-Black-Vault

http://www.dailymail.co.uk/news/article-5210245/Existence-UFOs-proved-reasonable-doubt.html

http://www.mirror.co.uk/science/more-thousand-new-galaxies-discovered-8442563

https://www.nytimes.com/2017/12/18/insider/secret-pentagon-ufo-program.html

https://www.scientificamerican.com/article/the-truth-about-those-alien-alloys-in-the-new-york-times-ufo-story/

https://www.livescience.com/20380-particles-quantum-tunneling-timing.html

https://phys.org/news/2014-05-scientists-year-quest.html

https://www.mnn.com/green-tech/research-innovations/stories/lightsabers-could-become-reality-after-incredible-physics

https://www.dailystar.co.uk/news/latest-news/705704/nasa-space-exploration-moon-earth-mars-jupiter-solar-system-galaxy-milky-way-aliens

http://www.bbc.com/news/science-environment-29093700

http://www.dailymail.co.uk/news/article-5906113/Secret-dossier-reveals-British-spies-spent-half-century-trying-catch-UFO.html?ITO=1490

https://www.dailystar.co.uk/news/world-news/683406/aliens-pentagon-united-states-space-washington-ufo-truth-nick-pope-james-oberg

http://www.redwoodfallsgazette.com/news/20170923/ghost-investigator-adrian-lee-now-claiming-ufo-sighting-in-redwood-falls

http://www.dailymail.co.uk/sciencetech/article-1299994/Churchill-Eisenhower-agreed-cover-UFO-encounter-WWII.html

http://www.dailymail.co.uk/news/article-2745169/Zombie-chic-Indonesian-village-Toraja-s-bizarre-annual-ritual-Ceremony-Cleaning-Corpses-MaiNene.html

https://phys.org/news/2014-05-scientists-year-quest.html#jCp

https://www.sciencealert.com/scientists-have-finally-discovered-massless-particles-and-they-could-radically-speed-up-electronics

http://mnmufon.org/mnmufon3_003.htm

http://www.ufoevidence.org/Cases/CaseSubarticle.
asp?ID=1012

https://www.experiencer.org/the-quantum-hologram-and-the-
nature-of-consciousness/

http://www.mirror.co.uk/news/technology-science/science/
heres-might-just-possible-escape-7092807

https://www.nsa.gov/public_info/_files/ufo/key_to_et_
messages.pdf. *NSA Technical Journal* Vol XIV No 1 with FOIA
Case number 41472 titled *Key to The Extraterrestrial Messages*. P
21.

Hanson, November. *Mosaic of the Extraterrestrial
Experience*. 2010. Pp54.

http://icar1.homestead.com/Mosaic_of_the_Extraterrestrial_
Final_Copy.pdf

http://www.nicap.org/images/humrep/JAR_2007_1st_Qtr1.
pdf

www. ufoabduction.com

http://www.jar-magazine.com/pdf-issues

Periodicals and Newspapers

McDonald, J. E. *UFOs over Lakenheath in 1956*. Flying
Saucer Review, Vol. 16, No. 2. 1970. pp 9-17.

Saint Paul Daily Globe, April 16, 1904.

Saint Paul Daily Globe, April 17, 1904. p 12.

Sauk Centre Herald, August 9, 1872.

Sauk Centre Herald, December 6, 1873.

Acknowledgements

To my mother, who warned me to be careful when I learned to juggle, as gangs of clowns always go for the juggler, and for the last time—there are no horses in horseradish sauce! To my father, putting on Halloween masks and throwing out made up gang signs will never be funny. To my sister Joanne, regardless of stealing and ruining my leather jacket in 1991 and for taking my heavy metal albums. And finally to Heather, Lorna, Jyeton, Kathy, Kevin, Scott, Gloria, and all at the The International Paranormal Society. I would like to thank those, deceased or living, who have contributed and made possible this paranormal adventure and put up with all my questions.

The following also supported me, kept me focused, and were there for me in various ways when I needed them: Paul, Karen, Ashley, Jordon, Nathan, Arloa, Stephen, Pat, Chad, Michelle, Chris, Gary, Ian, Rick, and all at Calumet Editions, and to all the small local historical societies that are reliant on the good will and charity of their members and volunteers to remain open and functioning as non-profit organizations. We all have a duty to make sure these buildings are still around for future generations to enjoy, long after we have departed ourselves.

About the Author

Adrian Lee is a historian and paranormal investigator who founded The International Paranormal Society. As the host of "More Questions than Answers," he reports on UFOs, ghosts, hauntings, and paranormal happenings around the world. He is also a psychic and has written the books: *How to be a Christian Psychic: What the Bible says about Mediums, Healers and Paranormal Investigators*; *Mysterious Midwest: Unwrapping Urban Legends and Ghostly Tales from the Dead*; and *Mysterious Minnesota: Digging Up the Ghostly Past at Thirteen Haunted Sites*.

Made in the USA
Monee, IL
17 April 2022

94648434R00166